# SAINT MOT
## OF CALCUTTA:
## A WITNESS TO LOVE

Michael J. Ruszala

Foreword...................................................................4

Introduction...............................................................7

Early Life in Skopje.....................................................11

The Sisters of Loreto...................................................17

A Pivotal Time for India ..............................................22

The Voice of Jesus ......................................................27

Preparation and Waiting ..............................................33

Into the Dark Holes of the Poor ...................................38

The Missionaries of Charity..........................................42

A Home for the Dying..................................................48

Growth of the Ministries..............................................52

All God's Children ......................................................56

Persuasion by Authenticity...........................................60

Making a Mark on the West.........................................64

The Pain of Longing ...................................................71

At Peace with the Darkness..........................................75

Mother Teresa's Message .............................................79

Opposition.................................................................83

Eternal Reward ..........................................................89

Conclusion.................................................................95

# Foreword

While the twentieth century was often a time of turbulence, selfishness, godlessness, and violence, Mother Teresa of Calcutta was a witness to love. She was a clear reminder of the goodness within human nature and the beauty of being truly open to God.

Officially proclaimed a saint in 2016, Mother Teresa (1910–1997) was a simple soul who opened her heart to others. She was filled with compassion for them and allowed herself to feel their pain, their loneliness, and their brokenness. In each person she met, Mother Teresa saw the image of her Lord, her Spouse. She reminds us of the dignity of each and every human life—that each life is unique and unrepeatable. Each life reflects its Creator and calls for a response of love. There is a beauty to the other-centeredness of Mother Teresa that calls out to be appreciated and imitated. This beautiful voice, calling us from its hiding place in the human heart, is not the voice of Mother Teresa, but of God.

'Mother' was her religious title, but as she ascended to the world stage, it became her role for the world—to be like a mother to all, no matter their origins. She was accepting and welcoming towards all people, not only towards the good or the like-minded. She continues to serve as an inspiration to people of all walks of life and all creeds. Where the world was blind to poverty and misery, Mother Teresa led the path to love.

Mother Teresa embraced India and its culture and people. Though criticized by some, she was a national heroine of great importance to the spirit of an independent India. She became one of them, dressed like them, and lived like them, all the while putting the timeless message of the gospel into practice.

Mother Teresa was also a witness to faith in action. She showed the vibrancy of faith and how it can touch the world around it for the better. Despite—and in fact because of—the long period of darkness she endured, Mother Teresa showed the world what it means to be an authentic believer. Her focus was on Christ, and the rest followed. She would go wherever he led her.

# Introduction

"If I ever become a Saint, I will surely be one of 'darkness'" (Kolodiejchuk, *Come Be My Light*, 1). Mother Teresa now is a saint, officially recognized by the Church. Despite years of experiencing feelings of emptiness, she was singly moved by her love of Christ her Spouse, whom she found in serving the "poorest of the poor." True meaning in life often evades people in our busy world; feelings of listless angst and the void are endured by the disenfranchised and forgotten among us, while they are simply covered over by many who are busy and productive. The 'useful' feel 'used,' the 'useless' feel like a burden. Qoheleth writes in the biblical book of Ecclesiastes, "I have seen all things that are done under the sun, and behold, all is vanity and a chase after wind" (Ecclesiastes 1:14). Everything changes. Everything passes. Only one thing remains—God.

For Mother Teresa, the rich and poor alike, the privileged and the forgotten, are both susceptible to great poverty, whether spiritual, emotional, or material. Hanging in torment on the cross, Jesus said, "I thirst" (John 19:28). His thirst was not for drink alone but especially for souls—to heal them, to save them, and to be united to them out of his great love. This was at the core of Mother Teresa's calling. Her spiritual director, Father Brian Kolodiejchuk, has come to believe that the darkness Mother Teresa experienced for so many decades was no ordinary doubt or depression, or even the 'dark night of the soul' experienced by holy souls, but rather a highly unique and heroic sharing in the sufferings of Christ and in the pain of the souls to whom she was sent to minister.

Mother Teresa advised that God calls us "not to be successful, but faithful." Most people engaged in charitable work would 'burn out' quickly after the satisfaction had ended and the miseries and troubles had become overwhelming—even more so because of terrible living conditions and non-existent pay. But Mother Teresa was not a social worker or a do-gooder, but a consecrated religious who remained madly in love with Jesus even when she did not feel his love in return. Hers was an unconditional love based on faith in God's unconditional love for her. She herself believed that only by the grace of such consecration and complete dedication could one endure such a life.

Mother Teresa was a genuine believer. Formerly atheist journalist Malcolm Muggeridge, in meeting Mother Teresa, saw in her what all the efforts in the world to maintain Christianity's relevance could not do (*Something Beautiful for God*, 31). In her was everything—the love, the faith, the trust, the single-heartedness. Only saints can show us that, and Mother Teresa was one of the prime examples of our time.

Still, because Mother Teresa made herself vulnerable to the world in serving the poorest of the poor, she was exposed to those who, unlike Malcolm Muggeridge, felt threatened by her work and ministry. Perhaps some saw in her a witness so powerful that it needed to be discredited to avoid a need for true conversion. Others, perhaps, saw a motive so foreign to the norm that it seemed like an anomaly. After all, Jesus himself was a controversial figure. The prophet Simeon said of him that he would be "a sign that will be contradicted" (Luke 2:34).

Mother Teresa was born Agnes Gonxhe Bojaxhiu in 1910 in Skopje, in modern-day Macedonia. She joined the Loreto Sisters in 1928, when she was only 18 years old. Desiring from a young age to be a missionary to India, she was soon sent from the motherhouse in Rathfarnham, Ireland, to Darjeeling, India, to complete the remainder of her formation. She took the religious name Teresa after St. Therese of the Child Jesus—the 'Little Theresa,' not the 'Big Theresa,' as she would say. Sister Teresa would serve many years as a teacher, and also a principal, in India with the Loreto Sisters.

Then in 1946, en route to her annual retreat in Darjeeling from Calcutta, she experienced locutions (inner voices) from Jesus, bringing about her "calling within a call" to satisfy his thirst for souls by serving among the "poorest of the poor." She could not do this as a Loreto sister, so she sought approval to form a new religious order, undergoing a very rigorous process of discernment under her spiritual director, the archbishop of Calcutta, the Holy See, and her religious superiors. Having submitted fully in her vow of obedience, she was permitted in 1948 to go out into the slums of Calcutta, after some brief preparation, wearing a white and blue sari as her religious habit.

The Congregation of the Missionaries of Charity was established in 1950 with 12 sisters, many of whom were former students of hers. They provided education for the poor, and love and medical care for those who would otherwise be abandoned, often giving them a sense of dignity and true acceptance in their last days.

In 1967, the journalist Malcolm Muggeridge of the BBC brought Mother Teresa's work to the world's attention. Mother Teresa was presented the Jawaharlal Nehru Award for

International Understanding by the Indian government in 1969 and the Nobel Peace Prize in 1979. The Missionaries of Charity, contemplatives in action among the poorest of the poor, grew to around 4,000 sisters by the time of Mother Teresa's death in 1997 and could be found all over the world. Mother Teresa, after a thorough investigation of her life and confirmation of the required miracles, was first beatified by Pope John Paul II in 2003 and then canonized a saint by Pope Francis in 2016. Officially known as St. Teresa of Calcutta, her feast day is September 5, and she is the patroness of World Youth Day and the Missionaries of Charity.

# Early Life in Skopje

When biographers came to Mother Teresa and asked about her childhood, she would not say much to them; she did not want people to focus on her own life but rather on "the work"—the work that God was doing with the poor. Her brother Lazar, however, was willing to provide some insightful anecdotes to biographers about her early life. Sometimes Mother Teresa would share a story or two herself, whether in a letter or in conversation.

Agnes Gonxhe Bojaxhiu, the future Mother Teresa, was born in Skopje in the Balkans on August 26, 1910, to Nikola and Drana Bojaxhiu, who had her baptized the very next day. It was that next day—her "true birthday"—that was all-important for Mother Teresa because it was the beginning of God's life of grace in her soul. In addition to her older brother Lazar, she had an older sister named Aga, who likewise became a religious sister, though in a different order. The children called their mother 'Nana Loke' which means 'mother of my soul.' Drana, or Nana Loke, was a wise and hardworking housewife and mother. Agnes was usually called 'Gonxhe' in her childhood—a name meaning 'rosebud.' Though sickly at times, she was a good child, small, round, and rosy-cheeked. She loved God, was helpful, obeyed her parents, and enjoyed reading.

Gonxha received her First Holy Communion at just the age of 5 ½, which was a powerful experience for her. She later said it was the beginning of her desire to bring souls to Jesus. While her older siblings would often sneak a snack during the fast before Communion, which was at that time from midnight on, Gonxha would never join them and always reminded them to keep the fast. Attending Catholic school at first at the parish of the Sacred Heart before having to attend public school later on, she was well liked by her classmates and had a happy home life.

Gonxha's family was Albanian, and they were not immune from the turbulent political events surrounding them. The Albanian people had lived under the dominion of the Turkish Ottoman Empire for many centuries. They often endured religious persecution for their Christianity, which in time led a majority of Albanians to yield to pressure from their overlords to convert to Islam (Greene, *Mother Teresa: A Biography*, 2–3). Gonxha's family was part of the Albanian Christian minority, and they were quite devout in their Catholicism. In the early 20th century, voices were growing louder for Albanian independence from the Ottoman Empire, an independence that was declared just two years after Gonxha's birth. Moved by the intransigence of the Young Turks then in power, several other ethnic states likewise declared independence from the Ottoman Empire, leading to the bloody Balkan Wars in 1912 and 1913. The conflict in the region ultimately helped spark World War I, which lasted from 1914 to 1918.

Skopje itself, now part of the Republic of Macedonia, was never part of Albania; Gonxha's father moved there for business reasons only a few years beforehand. Nikola was a part-owner of a construction business, known for building Skopje's first theater, and he provided well for his family. The Bojaxhiu family had a large home with enough land for some fruit trees. He was also politically involved, a supporter of Albanian independence, and was an outspoken member of the town council.

Everything changed for Gonxha and her family in 1919 when her father returned mysteriously ill after a political meeting in Belgrade. Her mother, Drana, frantically sent the eight-year-old Gonxha to find a priest to give her father Last Rites. Providentially, she found one just in time for him to receive the Anointing of the Sick. Shortly afterward, he died at the hospital—likely having been poisoned by his political enemies.

Gonxha's mother Drana was reduced to a stupor for months over her husband's death. The family was devastated not only emotionally but also financially. Nikola's brothers cheated the family out of Nikola's share of the business and his property assets other than the family home. Slowly recovering from the loss, Drana then worked hard to support the family with sewing jobs, but they were indeed very poor. The mother and her children were drawn closer than ever during this difficult time, and they turned ever more to their Catholic faith. They continued in their family tradition of praying the Rosary together each night, and sometimes Gonxha and her mother, who was an almost-daily communicant, would make a pilgrimage to the shrine of the Madonna of Letnice to pray for Our Lady's intercession. Gonxha also found solace in writing poetry. She was noted to be studious, mature, and well kept.

There was a great displacement of peoples because of the war, and, despite their hardship, Drana would turn away no one who asked for help regardless of their ethnic or religious background. Catholic, Orthodox, or Muslim didn't matter—everyone was a child of God. When anyone was hungry, she would take them in to feed them, and when her children would ask who they were, Drana would tell them they were family. Drana would not allow herself to become embittered against other groups because of her husband's apparent assassination. This likely made a strong impression on Gonxha, who would spend her life serving Christ in all peoples in their need, without regard for their ethnic or religious background.

Drana, or Nana Loke, would often take time to gather the children to share some words of wisdom, such as telling them always to help others when asked but never to advertise one's charitable actions to others. She had a knack for teaching moral anecdotes. Once she showed her children a basket of good apples and then put in a rotten apple. Within a few days, the whole basket was corrupted. This left an impression on the children that they must keep good company and influences.

Gonxha did not know any religious sisters, but felt at the age of twelve that she was called to give herself completely to God as a nun. Her mother pushed these impulses in her daughter aside for the time being, but they would be revisited within a few years, when the time was right. A dynamic Croatian Jesuit priest, Father Jambrekovic, was assigned to her parish, Sacred Heart Church. Gonxha joined the sodality he had founded to involve girls in devotions. There she was inspired by stories about missionaries, both current figures and heroes from the past, who spread God's love in the midst of sorry conditions in Bengal in India. Gonxha knew she wanted to be a religious sister on mission to India, so she spent much time in prayer and came to the decision to pursue this desire. When Gonxha told her mother, Drana was troubled and shut herself in her room to think and pray. When she came out the next morning, however, she encouraged her daughter to wholeheartedly follow God's call (Chawla, 5).

So Gonxha applied to be admitted to the Loreto Sisters, who worked with the Jesuits she had heard about in India. She was accepted for formation in Ireland first before being sent on to India to complete the rest of her formation and, ultimately, to serve there permanently. Gonxha, with tears in her eyes, boarded the train and said goodbye to her mother, whom she would never see again in this life. As she boarded, her mother told her, "Put your hand in His [Jesus'] hand, and walk alone with Him. Walk ahead, because if you look back you will go back" (*Come Be My Light*, 13). Gonxha, who was a skilled writer, drafted a poem around this time:

> I'm leaving my dear house

And my beloved land

To steamy Bengal go I

To a distant shore....

In return I ask only of Thee,

O most kind father of us all:

Let me save at least one soul—

One you already know... (*Come Be My Light, 16–17*).

# The Sisters of Loreto

Gonxha was only 18 when she set out on the train in the fall of 1928 to enter into religious life. Her immediate destination was Paris, where she would be interviewed before being sent on to the motherhouse in Rathfarnham, a suburb of Dublin, Ireland, to begin her postulancy with the Loreto Sisters. The Loreto Sisters, officially called the Institute of the Blessed Virgin Mary, were founded in England by Mary Ward in 1609 to focus on the great need for providing a Catholic education. The sisters were later invited to Ireland to teach there and then followed the Irish to India, where they established schools to serve Irish Catholics settling into those colonies, as well as the local peoples.

Gonxha spoke Albanian and Serbo-Croatian, neither of which the sisters understood. Her first interactions with the sisters had to be through a translator, so upon arriving in Ireland, she had to dedicate herself to immersion in English. Even when occupied with other work, Gonxha committed to learn ten new words a day. She would be expected to speak English from then on and ultimately to teach in the language as well. Her father learned a number of languages because of his many business travels, and Gonxha likewise picked up languages quickly. Gonxha spent just six weeks at Rathfarnham before being sent to her true destination: India. Becoming a teacher-missionary in India was what had attracted her to the Loreto Sisters in the first place—serving the poor, helping families step out of poverty through education, and showing students the love of Christ.

Gonxha set sail for India in December 1928 and arrived some weeks later in Bombay, where she got her first glimpse of the type of poverty she would later experience in India. She then traveled to the convent in Darjeeling, quickly learning the Bengali and Hindi languages. Darjeeling is in Bengal in northeastern India, in the foothills of the Himalayan Mountains. It used to be the summer vacation home of the viceroy of the British Raj, so it comprised many beautiful buildings and gardens and was the venue for many parades and events. It was also an educational center within India and a resort area for the wealthy. The Loreto Sisters accepted both rich and poor in their school. The rich paid tuition, and the poor did not have to pay, being subsidized by the tuition of the rich. Still, the schools where Gonxha was trained in teaching did not represent the abject poverty that she would experience in her future ministry outside the order.

Gonxha took her first vows of poverty, chastity, and obedience with the Loreto Sisters in 1931. She took the religious name

Mary Teresa after St. Therese of Lisieux, who was just recently canonized in 1925 and declared the patroness of missions in 1927. She chose the Spanish spelling 'Teresa' to distinguish herself from another sister in the order who was likewise named after St. Therese of Lisieux. St. Therese of Lisieux was a cloistered Carmelite nun who sought to please God not by doing great things, but by doing small things with great love. Dying of tuberculosis at the young age of 24, she offered these and many other daily sufferings for priests serving in the missions. St. Therese's 'Little Way' of small things with great love for God helps explain Mother Teresa's motivation in her works. The interior disposition of Christian love was the primary and guiding principle of her caring actions.

Sister Teresa's formation focused both on prayer and on mentoring for her work as a teacher. Afterwards, she was sent to be a teacher at Calcutta (today called Kolkata) at St. Mary's in the suburb of Entally, which encompassed a combination of both nicer neighborhoods and desperate slums. The Loreto Sisters had an enclosed complex in Entally with an ornate convent, beautiful grounds, and a large school with hundreds of students. The school was started as an orphanage, but the school had a variety of students—some were from wealthy families, some were from poor families or broken homes, and some were orphaned and living at the complex (Greene, 19). Paying students took classes in English while free students took classes in Bengali. Sister Teresa taught geography and history to the Bengali students, who remembered her as a great storyteller. In fact, the sisters called her the 'Bengali Teresa' because of her commitment to the Bengali speakers and to distinguish her further from the other sister, Sister Marie Therese Breen. Sister Teresa had a beautiful gift of laughter and would often place her hands on her hips when she laughed (Chawla, 15). The students also remember her as having great concern for their hygiene, because many of them did not have access to clean water. She would have them take baths and would give away bars of soap as prizes for good students—a rare luxury for some of them. Her fellow sisters remembered her as prayerful, punctual, and hardworking, as well as charitable and fair as a teacher. She always kept up with the rigorous schedule of the school while also attending to prayer. Moreover, the sisters noted her as being very ordinary and not drawing attention to herself.

In addition to having Loreto Sisters serving as teachers, St. Mary's also had Indian women from a congregation of the faithful as teachers. These women were in the beginning stages of forming a possible new religious order. They adopted a sari, a traditional Indian garment for women, as their distinctive religious garb. Sister Teresa would remember this years later when she formed the Missionaries of Charity and adopted the sari as a religious habit, showing a distinctively Indian mission.

Sister Teresa spent 17 fulfilling years at St. Mary's School. She became the principal in 1937, and in 1939 she took her final vows in the Institute of the Blessed Virgin Mary (the Sisters of Loreto), adopting the name Mother Teresa.

One student of hers later recalled, "I was a little nervous since I hadn't been to the city before and didn't know what to expect in this new school. All my fears melted away on meeting Mother. The day I joined school, Mother Teresa came into the parlor, called me by my name in such perfect Bengali, and greeted me in the Bengali way and language. What a welcome she gave me! Coming to know Mother over the next month, I came to appreciate her as more than a teacher or the headmistress" (Mother Teresa, *A Call to Mercy*, 156).

For most sisters, a full religious life served as an educator would have been more than enough. During this time, in addition to growing as an educator, Mother Teresa also grew in prayer. But further, she was soon to feel a call from God into the dark and the unknown, and into becoming a new type of missionary.

# A Pivotal Time for India

When Mother Teresa set foot in India for the religious life, she never looked back. She would become an Indian herself, and India would be her home for the rest of her life.

For centuries, India was under British control, which began with the dominance of the East India Company in the 18th century and was then carried over into the British Raj in the 19th century. Parts of India were well-maintained, though other parts were ignored, and the government's policies did not benefit the ordinary Indian. The population was massive, and so was the poverty of those particularly vulnerable to problems inevitably caused by wars, famine, and disease.

Traditional Hindu belief in the caste system further complicated the misery of the most vulnerable. Though the notion of 'untouchables' was gradually loosened in India in the early and mid-20th century, vestiges of the belief remained that, because of evil they must have done in past lives, this group of people were doomed to a miserable existence in this life. Thus, discrimination hampered the social mobility of millions of Indians, closing the door to education, healthcare, and gainful employment. Mother Teresa desired to serve not simply the poor but the "poorest of the poor." Many of these were so-called 'untouchables,' or *Dalits*.

By the early to mid-20<sup>th</sup> century, India was in the labor pains of the independence movement. India gradually moved towards autonomy after rebellions in the mid-19<sup>th</sup> century. The British considered partitioning the region on sectarian lines to facilitate their governance. The (Hindu) Indian National Congress and the Muslim League both stood strongly against the partition at first, and it was stalled in the early 1900s. Any partition would greatly disenfranchise the people and deprive many of their property and homes. The balance of power between the two groups was also of concern. India's involvement in the British war effort in World War I helped to further assert its place among the nations of the earth, and the British were gradually compelled to hand over more autonomy to the Indians.

A few years later, India also became involved in the war effort for Britain during World War II. The convent at St. Mary's in Entally was converted into housing for soldiers, so the sisters and the school were moved into temporary quarters in an old factory building during the war. War with the Japanese cut off much of India's supply of rice and resulted in the Bengal Famine of 1942–1943, in which millions perished. The streets of India were filled with homeless, starving people who had no medical attention. Food was hard to come by for Mother Teresa's schoolchildren as well, so one day in 1946 she went out to look for some. This was during the middle of violent chaos between Hindus and Muslims, and there were dead bodies out in the streets. The British military found Mother Teresa and told her to go home. She convinced them to bring a supply of food for her students and to give her a ride back to the school.

Following World War II, voices grew louder for complete independence. Greater steps towards autonomy by the British meant more power for the Hindu majority, and this angered the Muslims. So the British again considered partitioning the land, but the complications of who owned what land or who should live where fueled a cycle of violence and hatred between Hindus and Muslims that was beyond what the British could control. Thousands were killed in the violence and riots between Hindus and Muslims in India in the 1940s.

After all of the violence, many Hindu and Muslim leaders came to demand partition as the only way, despite Gandhi's insistence on a unified independent nation. With Britain's grasp of India weakening ever further, the colony was first partitioned into Hindu-majority India and Muslim-majority

Pakistan in 1947, which then included not only modern-day Pakistan to the west of India but also modern-day Bangladesh to the east of Bengal in India. India became independent in 1950, and Pakistan received its independence in 1956.

The partition of India in 1947 brought about the largest migration in human history, with millions of minorities fleeing their homes to live in the country that was controlled by their ethnic and religious majority. Setting fair terms for the partition was nearly impossible since any partition whatsoever would necessarily disenfranchise millions. In the end, 14 million people migrated to the other sides of the border. Those who did not were often chased out or killed by the majority population. Dead bodies in the streets were a common sight. Trains were packed with emigrants, who would even catch a ride on the roof of the cars since there was not enough space to stand inside. But even leaving on the train did not bring safety to some. Sometimes trains were attacked by rioters and the passengers were slaughtered out of revenge and ethnic hatred. Hundreds of thousands—perhaps even millions—died in the chaos and violence during the partition. Nationalism surged, and Ghandi himself was assassinated in 1948 for preaching peace over the excesses of Indian national pride.

India would become one of the great nations of the world, and its economy and social situation would gradually progress from this point in its history. Mother Teresa received full Indian citizenship in 1948. She wanted to become one with her people and to share in their common destiny as a nation. British colonialism had made outreaches such as the schools of the Loreto Sisters possible, but the current situation in India desperately required growth for new forms of ministries. Though Christianity was a small minority in India, her work and ministry would become intertwined with India's needs and growth and her care would be for any and all of India's people who might be in need. Though some locals at first distrusted her as a Christian foreigner, India's government would one day recognize her contributions to the nation in 1969 when it bestowed on her the Jawaharlal Nehru Award for International Understanding. Jawaharlal Nehru was the leader of the Indian National Congress who helped bring about India's full independence, then becoming the nation's first prime minister.

Yet as India itself was experiencing growing pains in the 1940s, Mother Teresa was about to experience them within herself as well.

# The Voice of Jesus

Mother Teresa was an ordinary sister in many respects, but because of her deep interior life, she was led to make a heroic personal vow in addition to the usual ones of poverty, chastity, and obedience. This vow was, under pain of mortal sin, to deny Jesus nothing that she felt he clearly asked of her (*Come Be My Light*, 31–32). In 1942, she submitted to her spiritual director her decision to make this vow and her feeling of being directed by God to do so. Because of her spiritual maturity, he allowed her to make it. There are many things that God may want us to do, but most people are willing to go about their business and ignore the invitation from God to do something out of the ordinary. But as Father Brian Kolodiejchuk, who led the cause of her canonization, points out, Mother Teresa wanted so much to please Christ her Spouse that she would refuse him nothing because he had refused her nothing. She would faithfully keep her vow, because unlike most people, she could not stand the thought of being even a moment in the state of mortal sin, separated from God's supernatural life in her soul. Father Kolodiejchuk believes God's inspiration for her to make this vow was what paved the way, primarily, for her to accept his call a few years later to move toward forming an order of sisters that would serve the poorest of the poor, and to stay heroically faithful the rest of her life.

In September 1946, Mother Teresa took her annual retreat. She took the train from Calcutta some 400 miles north to Darjeeling, to the Loreto convent. While on the train, she began to experience locutions. In other words, she would hear a clear, interior voice, from Jesus. He called for her to satisfy his thirst for souls by serving the poorest of the poor and to take his love to them in their hovels. In a clear voice within herself, he spoke to her tenderly as a spouse and enjoined her, "Come, be my light." Father Kolodiejchuk writes, "With utmost tenderness, He [Jesus] addressed her as '*My own* spouse' or '*My little one.*' 'My Jesus' or My own Jesus,' replied Mother Teresa, longing to return love for love" (*Come Be My Light*, 44). These locutions continued throughout her retreat. On three occasions, she also had visions—two visions of the poor and one of Jesus on the cross with his Mother standing below (*Come Be My Light*, 101).

While dying on the cross, Jesus in the Gospel said, "I thirst." Nothing that the Gospels record from Calvary is trivial; rather, every passage is of great significance to salvation. Jesus' thirst was not only for drink, therefore, but for souls. Mother Teresa understood that this meant Jesus did not merely love souls but longed for them desperately. It pained him to be separated from them. Mother Teresa was filled with a longing to satisfy this desire of Jesus, who so tenderly gave his life for us. Mother Teresa loved her life and work as a religious with the Loreto order and was not eager to leave them except at God's calling. In fact, she later spoke of her leaving them as a sacrifice even greater for her than leaving her family for the religious life. She was obedient to the Voice, however, and longed also to satisfy it. This, rather than witnessing the suffering of the poor and thinking of what to do about it, was her primary inspiration to go out and do the kind of work that many would think devoid of hope for success.

Later, after founding the Missionaries of Charity, Mother Teresa referred to August 10 as 'Inspiration Day,' which was celebrated by the order. But she never told her sisters about the locutions from Jesus. She did tell them that it was the day she was inspired to satisfy the dying Jesus' thirst for souls by serving him in the distressing disguise of the poorest of the poor. When she returned from her retreat, however, she fully recounted her experience to her spiritual director, Father Celeste Van Exem, a Jesuit, along with the notes she had written concerning the Voice. The account of the locutions would only become public during her process for sainthood, after her death.

Father Van Exem was not unmoved by Mother Teresa's account of hearing the Voice of Jesus, but he was also a prudent spiritual director, formed in distinguishing the will of God from one's own will or even the suggestions of the Devil. After carefully listening to her account, Father Van Exem forbade her to think about it ever again. This was certainly a very difficult cross for Mother Teresa, but if she were a true bearer of a message from God, she would follow God's will first in obeying her superiors. She, of course, did not realize at the time that the command from her spiritual director was simply part of a strategy of discernment. Mother Teresa asked for permission to speak to the archbishop about the Voice, but Father Van Exem would not permit her. So she obeyed the best she could to stop thinking about it. After several months, Father Van Exem was satisfied that Mother Teresa had shown she was first of all willing to obey the will of God as expressed through her superiors, and letting God do as he willed with his extraordinary message. So Father Van Exem approached her once again, in January 1947, granting her permission to write to Archbishop Ferdinand Perier of Calcutta.

Meanwhile, some other sisters, unaware of what was going on in Mother Teresa's soul, noticed that she was spending an unusually long time in confession with Father Van Exem. They complained to mother provincial about what they saw as an inappropriate relationship with a priest. Mother Teresa, who was the principal of St. Mary's, was consequently reassigned in January 1947 to the Loreto convent at Asensol, 140 miles northwest of Calcutta, even though it was the middle of the school year. Mother Teresa submitted without complaint. She did not even explain the reason for her consultation with Father Van Exem since she was ordered to silence over her locutions from Jesus. Instead, Mother Teresa welcomed the change as a providential opportunity for more prayer, since though she would be teaching, she would fewer administrative responsibilities. Mother Teresa would later be cleared of suspicion by the superior general in Ireland and send back to her beloved St. Mary's for the following school year, though not as principal since a new one was in place.

Archbishop Perier, a Jesuit like Father Van Exem trained in discernment of God's will, was even more cautious in handling the matter of Mother Teresa's extraordinary call. He did not dismiss her, but he made her wait. Meanwhile the Voice continued and the urgency within her to satisfy it intensified. Mother Teresa wrote many letters to the archbishop, and Father Van Exem wrote to him on her behalf as well. But while reading her letters with interest, Archbishop Perier would not move in granting any consent for her to leave the convent to serve in the slums. Mother Teresa did not realize, however, that the archbishop was discussing the matter behind the scenes with important experts to see what should be done. She was quite persistent in writing him, trying to urge him to move and even praying for his change of heart, but she always respected his authority and never violated it.

Through the tough questions he proposed to her in his return letters, the archbishop was also helping her to refine and hone the mission of this new congregation that would soon emerge (*Come Be My Light*, 55). If she were to leave the convent, she would also be departing from the structure of the Loreto sisters, though she earnestly desired to remain in religious life. She believed that only the grace of the consecration and total commitment of religious life could enable one to do the kind of hard and thankless lifelong work she desired to do among the poorest of the poor. Only their strong interior life could be expected to prevail in such difficult circumstances, from which most people would shy away.

She would also have to show Archbishop Perier how her new congregation would be fulfilling a role that no other existing order or congregation could then fill. Since there were so many women's religious orders at the time, any bishop would have to demonstrate to Rome how a new order to be approved was altogether unique in its mission. What would be specific about this new congregation, the Missionaries of Charity, would be that they would be one with those they served. They would be specifically Indian among the Indians, specifically very poor among the very poor. They would even dress like them, speak their language, eat the same foods, and sleep in the same types of dwellings. As Christ had become one of us in all things but sin, they would become one of them, and win them by love and trust. No other order was so closely identified with the people they served. The Loreto sisters wore European habits, dwelt behind secure walls, and lived a European-style lifestyle. Other orders served the poor, but in more institutionalized settings modeled after Europe. The Missionaries of Charity, even when they would someday reach beyond India, would adopt the culture and language of whatever people they served. Thus, Mother Teresa left colonization behind entirely and focused exclusively on evangelization within a new cultural setting. Their charism would be to satisfy the thirst of Jesus in the poorest of the poor.

# Preparation and Waiting

Having prayed and consulted trusted advisors, Archbishop Perier invited Mother Teresa to write to the mother superior of the Loreta Sisters in Ireland for her permission. He supervised Mother Teresa in writing her letter and insisted that she request secularization rather than exclaustration as Mother Teresa had desired (Chawla, 24). While exclaustration would permit her to be a sister of Loreto outside the convent, secularization would disassociate her from the order itself. The mother superior took only one month to respond. The mother superior gave her a favorable response, and even though the letter from Mother Teresa requested secularization (despite her true desire at the time to remain part of Loreto), the mother superior insisted on exclaustration—for her to do her work outside the convent and the norms while remaining a sister of Loreto. Mother Teresa surely saw this as providential and a blessing for her leap of faith. The mother superior knew that some others in the order would not look favorably on Mother Teresa's plans, so she ordered her to speak of it to none of her other superiors.

With the mother superior's approval secured, Archbishop Perier and Father Van Exem helped Mother Teresa to write to the Vatican at Rome to seek the final approval necessary. But

Archbishop Perier again insisted that the request to Rome be that of secularization. She sent her petition to Rome in February 1948, and then waited for many long months without any sign of a reply. Finally, in July, Archbishop Perier received word from Rome. He notified Father Van Exem, who then told Mother Teresa that Rome had made its decision. She did not want to hear the outcome until she first spent some time in prayer. Then Father Van Exem told her: whereas the eventual founder of the Loreto Sisters, Mary Ward, had petitioned Rome unsuccessfully for a similar purpose some centuries ago, this time Rome granted exclaustration to Mother Teresa. This is what she truly wanted (even though she was not allowed to ask for it), and was yet another confirmation that her new calling was most certainly God's will.

In August 1948, Mother Teresa put out three saris, purchased for just one rupee, with a cross and rosary for Father Van Exem to bless (Greene, 24). These saris were white, edged with three blue lines: blue for Mary and three for the religious vows of poverty, chastity, and obedience. They would serve as her new religious habit. In fact, each Missionary of Charity would someday be given just three saris for her use at one time—one to wear, one to wash, and one to mend. For hygienic purposes, washing would be necessary every day. Mother Teresa did not put the sari on just then, but when Father Van Exem saw Mother Teresa wearing one of the saris a few months later, he didn't even recognize her! Only Indian women wore those types of saris, and she truly looked like one of them. Mother Teresa's saris were in fact similar to the garments worn by the workers who cleaned the streets.

Mother Teresa had kept silence so well that this was the first time her fellow sisters heard of her intentions. Some sisters thought it was a heroic work of love. Others considered it a foolish move destined for nothing but failure. So the superiors put out a memo to the Loreto sisters throughout India that during this time, the sisters should neither praise nor criticize Mother Teresa, but should only pray for her.

Mother Teresa wrote to her mother Drana to let her know about her lawfully leaving the Loreto Sisters to serve the poor while still remaining in the religious life. It would be the last time she would have the opportunity to correspond with her mother for over a decade because of the coming 'Iron Curtain' in Communist Albania. During that time, Drana came to assume that her daughter was dead. She was overjoyed to hear again from her daughter after the situation in Albania opened up to some extent. Drana would live until 1971, and Mother Teresa would at last come to visit her grave in 1990.

Father Van Exem's prudence would not allow Mother Teresa to simply go out unprepared into the chaos of the slums, and Archbishop Perier was in agreement (Chawla, 27). They arranged for her to receive some medical training from the Medical Mission Sisters at Patna, around 350 miles northwest of Calcutta. The senior girls from St. Mary's loved Mother Teresa and gathered in hopes of catching her to say goodbye as she set off. But they missed her as she went out, dressed in a sari in the dark of late evening. Many of Mother Teresa's friends send her letters at Patna, wishing her well and assuring her of their prayers. Having the prayers of so many with her was an encouragement to Mother Teresa.

The sisters in Patna, who served the poor who were brought to their makeshift hospital, were trained as nurses and surgeons. At Patna, Mother Teresa was immediately immersed in observing and assisting with a whole host of common and uncommon emergencies, diseases, and conditions. Focused and attentive despite any difficulty, one of her greatest joys was assisting with childbirth. The sisters also gave her much valuable, practical information concerning hygiene, nutrition, and medical care, and the superior of the Medical Missionary Sisters, Mother Anna Dengal, gave her many tips she would use in setting the groundwork for the Missionaries of Charity. She also gave advice, based on science and experience, for what could be humanly expected of Mother Teresa's future sisters serving the poorest of the poor (Greene, 35).

Yearning to answer the call of Jesus, Mother Teresa wrote multiple times to Father Van Exem to let her get to the "real work." Naturally, he thought she needed more time in training. He came to Patna a bit later to check up on her. By that time, she had been there about four months. He asked several leaders of the facility if she thought Mother Teresa had enough medical training to be ready to begin her work. They all said she was ready enough. She knew what to do, or at least where to find help when needed. So he let her go to begin a work so filled with danger, yet which she so desired to do.

# Into the Dark Holes of the Poor

Mother Teresa, however, was not allowed to stay with the Sisters of Loreto during her new mission. The superior general insisted that Loreto facilities be kept only for the Loreto mission. After searching a while for a suitable place to stay, Mother Teresa was ultimately taken in by the Little Sisters of the Poor, who ran a home for the elderly. It was a good arrangement for her because they kept a strict adherence to living in poverty and likewise worked among the poor, though in a different way. Upon arriving, she spent eight days in prayer before setting out for the slums. The Sisters of Loreto, to whom she was still attached, gave her a small allotment of money. They would have given her more, but Mother Teresa insisted on relying on providence (Chawla, 37).

Mother Teresa set her sights on Motijhil, a slum that she used to see from her window at St. Mary's. Whereas Motijhil would later become a decent place to live, in 1948 it was flooded over with misery from the tumultuous events of the 1940s. Motijhil, which means 'Pearl Lake,' was situated around a stinking cesspool. Garbage was piled up on the sides of the streets, and homeless and hopeless people were stretched out everywhere.

But Father Van Exem thought she should begin with a less difficult challenge—Taltala, where some of her students from St. Mary's lived. It was hard enough to begin with. Mother Teresa set out for Taltala on the morning of December 21, 1948, accompanied by a companion. She wrote of that experience, "We started at Taltala and went to every Catholic family. The people were pleased, but children were all over the place, and what dirt and misery, what poverty and suffering. I spoke very, very little, I just did some washing of sores, and dressings, gave medicine to some" (*Come Be My Light*, 132). Mother Teresa also encountered a poor woman dying on the street and tried to do what little she could.

Mother Teresa went on to Motihjil, talking to parents of children, telling them of her intentions of starting a school right there in Motijhil. Many were enthusiastic about it as there were no other opportunities for advancement available to their children. The next morning, there were five children waiting for her to teach them. Mother Teresa started with the Bengali alphabet. She had no blackboard, so she just wrote in the dirt. Looking back, she would often say that the Missionaries of Charity literally began on the ground. Soon the sounds of children chanting their alphabet was a common sound in Motijhil as more and more children joined. Soon, she had 56 students before her. She would beg for food to feed them and, like at St. Mary's, would give out bars of soap as rewards, having the children take baths and practice hygiene.

Some people she approached for help were generous. Others threw only insults in her direction. The blow that hurt her the most, however, was when she went to see a nearby parish priest who treated her harshly and turned her away as a troublemaker. Passing that way often brought tears to her eyes. Soon into her arrival in the slums, God's special consolations to her vanished and she entered what she later called "the dark night of the birth of the society." Difficulty, rejection, and loneliness set in. She thought often of going back to Loreto, where she did not have to endure the insults, misery, and uncertainties of the slums. In fact, the mother provincial often asked her to consider coming back. But Mother Teresa persevered. Actually, the hardships facing Mother Teresa's soul would never abate, despite future successes in her ministry. But her faith kept her going, knowing that Jesus had called her to satisfy his thirst for souls in the poorest of the poor. Despite the tears, Mother Teresa kept her joy. For Mother Teresa, joy isn't a mood but a state of the soul, knowing the goodness of God. St. Paul tells us in the Bible, "Rejoice in the Lord always. I shall say it again: rejoice!"

(Philippians 4:4). Mother Teresa always insisted that her future sisters live in this joy and share it with others.

Mother Teresa sought help from another pastor, and he gave her some money. She used that money to rent two huts—one to house her school and one to house the sick and dying whom she found on the streets. Many dwellers at Motijhil gave her what little extra furniture they could spare. Soon she had tables for her school, which she named Nirmal Hriday, Home of the Pure Heart. She later gave that name to her dispensary for the sick.

Within a month, Mother Teresa had attracted a number of lay volunteers to help with the work, including some teachers from St. Mary's. Within a month and with the help of the lay volunteers, she was able to open even another school in a nearby slum that was even worse off than Motijhil. She would often remind her helpers with five fingers of the reason for their service to the poor: "you–did–it–to–Me"—a reference to the words of Jesus in the Gospel of Matthew (Matthew 25:40).

Archbishop Perier acted as her superior during those first years. He asked her to keep a written record of her progress and activities among the poor, since at the end of her year of exclaustration, her work would be reviewed and she would have to apply to Rome for an extension until her new order was approved. Upon reviewing her work and given the archbishop's strong recommendation, Rome, after another long delay, gave her an extension of three years.

# The Missionaries of Charity

In 1949, Mother Teresa moved to the empty upper floor of a family residence at 14 Creek Lane since she needed to be closer to Motijhil. It was owned by two brothers, one of whom did some work for Father Van Exem and gladly offered lodging to Mother Teresa at no cost. Little by little, Mother Teresa's new order was becoming a reality, yet she had no sisters. She prayed, trusting God through Mary's intercession. The first two girls who came to join Mother Teresa in the religious life came soon after she moved to 14 Creek Lane, and were both former students of hers. A Bengali girl named Subashini, whom Mother Teresa had taught from the seventh grade, understood her teacher's passion. Mother Teresa would encourage some of her students even then to go visit the sick and lonely in the hospitals of the city. Subashini, a petite and mild-mannered girl whom Mother Teresa described as pure-hearted, became Sister Agnes. Then another student, Magdalena, tall and extraverted, came to 14 Creek Lane to join Mother Teresa. She became Sister Gertrude, a doctor for the poor.

Within two to three years, there would be 27 sisters living on the upper floor at 14 Creek Lane. Archbishop Perier charged Father Van Exem with drafting the constitution of the new order, which he patterned especially after Mother Teresa's notes from the Voice that inspired her to satisfy the thirst of Jesus by serving the poorest of the poor. Then in 1950, Rome fully approved the Missionaries of Charity as a new religious order in the Catholic Church, under the guidance of the Archdiocese of Calcutta. Archbishop Perier came to 14 Creek Lane on October 7 to officially proclaim the start of the new archdiocesan congregation—the Congregation of the Missionary Sisters of Charity. He also proclaimed its purpose, "To quench the thirst of Our Lord Jesus Christ for the salvation of souls by the observance of the three Vows of Poverty, Chastity and Obedience, and of an additional fourth Vow to devote themselves with abnegation to the care of the poor and needy who, crushed by want and destitution, live in conditions unworthy of the human dignity" (*Come Be My Light*, 139).

It was a joy to Mother Teresa to see Jesus' wish being fulfilled. Archbishop Perier granted Mother Teresa another holy desire: permission to house the Blessed Sacrament in their own chapel. She felt now that with Jesus' Real Presence, she and the sisters could accomplish anything for him. She spent the whole day in Adoration of the Eucharist. The Missionaries of Charity were dedicated to the Immaculate Heart of the Blessed Virgin Mary. Praying the Rosary was dear to Mother

Teresa, who thumbed her rosary constantly as a connection to the Blessed Mother. She made it part of the rules of the order that the sisters must not go out to the slums before having said prayers asking for Mary's intercession. In fact, the sisters would even count distances by how many Rosaries they could pray along the way!

Mother Teresa formed her sisters to be both active and deeply contemplative—not only to work but also to dedicate themselves deeply to prayer. Prayer would sustain their difficult life of action and would enable them to be instruments of God among the poor. Her sisters began their novitiate on April 11, 1951, and she was very happy with their spiritual progress. Her aim was to become a saint and for her sisters to become saints as well, since this would be pleasing to God. It was not so much what they would accomplish in the world, but how much love they poured into what little work they could do. Mother Teresa's first sisters then took their first vows in the order—poverty, chastity, obedience, and the extra vow of free and willing service to the poorest of the poor—on April 12, 1953, as Mother Teresa took her final vows.

Many girls and young women were attracted to Mother Teresa and the important work she was doing—work that they knew all too well needed to be done. They were also moved by Mother Teresa's ardent longing to satisfy Jesus' thirst for souls, and wanted to join her in this permanently as sisters. Many came directly from St. Mary's School. Even some teachers and Loreto Sisters joined Mother Teresa. While Mother Teresa did not actively recruit anyone to leave Loreto or St. Mary's, many of the remaining Loreto Sisters began to feel very bitterly towards Mother Teresa for taking away vocations that could have gone to Loreto (*Come Be My Light*, 137). Mother Teresa was deeply wounded by this since she loved Loreto and because many of her detractors were friends of hers. Mother Teresa wrote to the mother provincial to show that she meant no ill and to assure the sisters that she would not make any active attempt to take away Loreto vocations. The mother provincial did her best to rectify a charitable disposition within the community at Loreto. It would take some time, but eventually the relationship between the Loreto Sisters and the Missionaries of Charity would be restored.

Sister Mary Perma, the present-day superior general of the Missionaries of Charity, remembers what it was like to be received into formation by Mother Teresa at a later point in the order's history: "I remember Mother from the time I joined the society... In the little prayer service, she fixed the little shoulder cross for us, she gave us Rosary, and with that, the first steps in the religious life were taken. And Mother was very attentive to our own mothers who had accompanied us, and profusely she thanked them and said, 'Thank you for giving your daughters to God and to our society.' And our mothers also went away consoled" (ShalomWorldTV).

As the mother superior of the Missionaries of Charity, Mother Teresa radiated joy and love to the sisters but also called them out to a high standard of holiness. Sister Mary Perma recalls, "Mother was very strong in her convictions and very fast in what she discovered to be the will of God.... And on the other hand, Mother was very tender, very sweet, very humorous, especially with us in the community. She enjoyed being with us, and we enjoyed being with Mother. She would care for us and give little special attention knowing what the sister's special likings would be. She would attend to that" (ShalomWorldTV).

But one of the first women who earnestly wanted to join Mother Teresa in her work was prevented from doing so when she developed a debilitating condition. Jacqueline de

Decker, likewise dressed in a sari, had come from a wealthy family in Belgium to serve Jesus in the poor in India. A Jesuit priest directed Miss de Decker to Mother Teresa, who was then in 1948 receiving medical training in Patna. Sure enough, the two struck up a strong friendship. Sadly, symptoms of severe back pain Miss de Decker was experiencing led way to partial paralysis. She had to return to Belgium and would undergo several dozen operations. She had to wear a neck brace for the rest of her life and continued to endure much pain and as a result of her condition. Mother Teresa called Miss de Decker her 'second self' and corresponded with her often. Despite Miss de Decker's great disappointment at not being able to join Mother Teresa in her work, Mother Teresa told her that if she offered her suffering up to God for the work, she would be a true collaborator.

This was the beginning of what the Vatican would later recognize in 1969 as the International Association of Co-Workers of Mother Teresa (Chawla, 102). Over the years, Miss de Decker would attract and organize thousands to join, and Mother Teresa would keep in touch with them via newsletter, forming them to collaborate well. To this day, anyone, Catholic or otherwise, willing to commit themselves to the service of the poor in their daily lives may join, after contacting a

Missionaries of Charity house. According to the association's website, "A co-worker of Mother Teresa is one who sees the presence of God in every human being and choose [sic] to fully share in the real service of the poor using hands to serve and hearts to love. Mother Teresa desired her Co-Workers to maintain deep family love in their own homes, and beyond that, to seek to serve those in need in their own neighbourhood, their town, their country, the world" (colaboradores.org). In many cases, co-workers provide material help to the Missionaries of Charities, including much-needed work and supplies. Others, like Jacqueline de Decker, remain at home, offering their prayers, love, and sacrifices to God for the work.

# A Home for the Dying

The Missionaries of Charity were growing fast, attracting young women with their radical authenticity and love of Jesus in the poor. They were becoming a regular sight in Calcutta as well. Mother Teresa's biographer Navin Chawla, a Hindu, writes, "even in the meanest of streets of Calcutta, the Sisters need no protection. They are recognized from afar, and wherever they go they are respected. The underlying reason is that they are as poor as anyone else and treat the poor as their equals" (66).

Mother Teresa and her sisters came upon many unfortunate people dying alone in the streets under miserable conditions. Often they were covered in maggots or nibbled on by rats. People would almost step over them as they went on their way. Hospitals would not take patients who either could not pay or who could not be successfully cured. Mother Teresa and her sisters tried to get many of them admitted to hospitals, but often they could not. Meanwhile, the huts that Mother Teresa was renting could house only a handful of patients.

So Mother Teresa approached the city government for assistance. Dr. Ahmed, the chief medical officer, proposed letting her use an abandoned pilgrims' hostel for the Kali

Temple in the Kalighat section of Calcutta (Chawla, 160). Mother Teresa liked the site and found it to be suitable for her need. She opened there in August 1952, naming it Nirmal Hriday, Pure Heart, in honor of the Immaculate Heart of Mary. It is still in operation to this day as the first dispensary of the Missionaries of Charity. The dispensary was for all those who could not be admitted to hospitals, and was offered free of charge. There was a large room for men and one for women, each with about 60 small cots. The sisters and helpers would provide love and kindness to the patients and would wash their sores, remove maggots, and provide basic medicine as needed. One patient is quoted as saying, "I lived like a dog. Now I die like an angel!" Since a great many of the patients were terminally ill, bodies were placed in a partitioned section before funeral rites.

The nearby Kali Temple in Kalighat was a major religious attraction in India. The goddess Kali attracted devotion from many Hindu believers as a motherly figure and protector. According to Hindu myth, the multi-armed Kali was a warrior against the forces of evil. She committed suicide after a slight against her husband, and the god Vishnu threw a discus at her body, which then shattered into pieces. The Kali Temple was built on the site where the pieces of Kali's body were supposed to have come to rest. Consequently, many Indians chose the Kali Temple in Kalighat as the place for their funeral rites and cremation.

Mother Teresa hence found it fitting that her dispensary for the dying be, as it turned out, nearby this site connected to the Hindu consciousness of the rites of passing from this life. But many Hindus did not see it that way. They saw Nirmal Hriday as a threat to Hinduism and a slight to the goddess Kali, both because the mission was Christian and because the Hindu priests said the site was said to be too holy to be occupied by the dying. Mother Teresa, however, respected the religious rites of the patients, offering water from the Ganges to dying Hindus, reading passages of the Quran to Muslims, and providing for Catholics to receive the sacrament of the sick (Greene, 70). As for the dying, for Mother Teresa, death was really birth to new life, and was sacred.

Locals, pilgrims, and Hindu priests came to protest outside Nirmal Hriday in its early days. A police officer entered the facility and found Mother Teresa tenderly caring to the wounds of poor Hindus. He came out and told the crowd that he would evict Mother Teresa only when the women of the neighborhood would come forward to carry on the wonderful work she was doing. They dispersed. Later on, many of the Hindu priests came to accept the presence of the Missionaries of Charity after one of their fellow priests fell ill and was rejected by the hospitals. He received honorable care at Nirmal Hriday, in keeping with his customs and best interests (Greene, 71).

The biographer Navin Chawla remarked, "For her, this was all the manifestation of either the dying Christ—so this was her God—or the abandoned Christ, or the suffering Christ. So she saw everyone from the prism of her religion, but she didn't discriminate" ("Nirmal Hriday" documentary). Sister Mary Perma explains how the Missionaries of Charity often bring God into situations without preaching: people "look at us and watch, more than our words, which in many places we cannot say. They see what we are doing, and it gives them confidence" (ShalomWorldTV).

# Growth of the Ministries

The Missionaries of Charity were outgrowing their upper-room beginnings. They needed a whole building of their own. In answer to her prayers, a mysterious man knocked on the door at 14 Creek Lane and offered to show Mother Teresa a building that was for sale. It was a three-story building, and the address was 54A Lower Circular Road. After leading Mother Teresa to the property, the man vanished. Mother Teresa found the property suitable to her needs and spoke to the owner, Dr. Islam, about the work of the Missionaries of Charity who would be living there. The owner, a Muslim man, was very moved by what he heard. He contacted the archbishop and ultimately sold him the building at a very low price for the use of the Missionaries of Charity. The sisters moved there in February 1953, and from then on, 54A Lower Circular Road known as 'Motherhouse.' The Missionaries of Charity were responsible paying off the cost of the property, and they were able to do so in a short period of time. Lower Circular Road, a busy thoroughfare in the city, was later renamed A. J. C. Bose Road.

Motherhouse would soon become a center of prayer and a hub of activity for the sisters, who would grow there to several hundred in number. Mother Teresa chose to maintain an austere condition for the building in solidarity with the poor.

As with all future houses of the Missionaries of Charity, the words "I thirst" were inscribed over the cross in the chapel, and the sisters would sit on the floor to pray. The only fan in the building was for visitors, toward the entrance. Meals were cooked over a charcoal fire, just as the poor would do. Sisters went early to bed and then would rise at 5 a.m. to allow time for Mass and prayers before taking the common van or walking to their places of ministry in the city at 8 a.m., going out like Jesus' disciples in groups of two. All the sisters would be back to Motherhouse by 1 p.m. for lunch. They would then return to their work in the city before returning by 6 p.m. for dinner and Adoration of the Blessed Sacrament.

All meals had to be at the Motherhouse. This kind of rule had its basis in ancient monastic practices but also took on new practical meaning for their work. The poor would want to repay the sisters out of what little they had, while the rich would offer them from their abundance. Mother Teresa wanted to offend no one or refuse no one while accepting from another, so she made it a rule not to accept food or drink for oneself from anyone, whether rich or poor. The sisters ate in common and carried drinking water with them as they went out. Even when Mother Teresa would go to meet with very important official, she would not so much as accept a cup of tea.

The sisters came across many people in the streets with leprosy. The infectious ailment, known now as Hansen's disease, is caused by bacteria that erodes the skin and tissue, producing fearsome and debilitating results. Though deadly if allowed to run its course, leprosy is now treatable. Still, it carried with it, as ever, a great social stigma. Caring for those suffering from leprosy certainly had its challenges, simply from a social standpoint. Firstly, other patients at dispensaries were very fearful of patients with leprosy and did not want to be near them. Secondly, many suffering with leprosy were physically unable or afraid to go out for treatment, even if it were provided free. So Mother Teresa acquired vans to serve as mobile leprosy treatment centers. These blue vans became frequent and welcome sights in the city, bringing hope and treatment to those suffering from leprosy. The bell was traditionally the symbol of leprosy, giving warning to others of their approach. The vans now used the bell to announce hope through their presence in the area.

While some people suffering from leprosy lived with their families, who were then at risk for the disease themselves, others were ostracized and lived together in the worst places imaginable. Mother Teresa realized that she needed a home for those suffering from leprosy. The Missionaries of Charity put forth a campaign in the city to "Touch the Leper with Your Compassion," which was well-received and brought in donations of money and supplies for the leprosy community. She approached the local government with a request for land. Navin Chawla, her future biographer, served a government official and worked with the governor. Mother Teresa approached him with a request to see the governor to talk about the desperate needs of the leprosy population in the area and to ask for five acres of land for them. He brought Mother Teresa in to see the governor, who was deeply moved by her appeal. Navin Chawla recalls when the governor asked her how much land she wanted. Seeing that he was so amenable, "She looked at me with a smile and she looked at the governor and she said, 'Ten acres.' He gave her eleven acres" ("Nirmal Hriday: Home of the Pure of Heart" Government of India documentary). This was Navin Chawla's first encounter with Mother Teresa.

As a result, Mother Teresa founded the City of Peace at Titlagargh. The quarter, which previously had been overrun with crime, was slowly transformed into something beautiful

(Chawla, 138). Missionaries of Charity brothers, who were now the men's branch of the order founded in 1954, together with able-bodied leprosy patients themselves, helped to construct this 'city' for the leprosy community, which was completed in 1968 after a decade of work. There, they received the treatments that modern medicine could provide. Those no longer infectious were employed to produce the blue and white saris for the Missionaries of Charity as well as their bed sheets. They were treated with dignity and were able to put their abilities to use while receiving treatment. Mother Teresa opened up many more centers for those suffering with leprosy in India and abroad in the coming years.

# All God's Children

Mother Teresa began her work opening a school for the children of the slums, but she soon saw that an even more immediate need was simply food, shelter, and love for the many orphaned children abandoned on the streets. After approval from the city, she opened up her first Shishu Bhavan or Children's Home of the Immaculate Heart, in September 1955. It was in a small house a short walk from the Motherhouse. The need for such an orphanage was great. Many babies and infants were abandoned, and the sisters would go out and bring them to the home. They would tend to their hygiene, give them much-needed medical care, food, and love. Within a few years, the sisters needed more facilities for the many abandoned children in need of care. The children's homes were bright and happy places, friendly to children. Adoption carried with it a social stigma in India at the time, but Mother Teresa's efforts helped make it commonplace and widely accepted. The sisters would facilitate adoption and were very careful to provide good and wholesome home environments for her children. As a rule, they would place children only with married couples. In some cases, the sisters would provide permanent care.

Mother Teresa was also an outspoken against abortion. Abortion, the killing of the unborn, was not the answer to the poverty in India. Instead, it was another injustice against the 'unwanted' of society and perpetuated a culture of violence. The mother and the father must both accept the gift of each child and open themselves to love, making the sacrifices necessary to welcome this new person created in the image of God. Adoption was the alternative she offered to abortion for those unable to keep the child. She would welcome the children and give them a good home.

Mother Teresa was saddened by a different kind of poverty in the developed world. She came to speak of a poverty beyond material poverty that she saw in the West. She said, "There are many in the world who are dying for a piece of bread but there are many more dying for a little love. The poverty in the West is a different kind of poverty—it is not only a poverty of loneliness but also of spirituality. There's a hunger for love, as there is a hunger for God" (Mother Teresa, *A Simple Path*).

Mother Teresa could accommodate the children who came her way, but with new secularized laws regarding adoption, the Missionaries of Charity were faced with new dilemmas some time after Mother Teresa's passing. In 2015, some 17 years after Mother Teresa's death, the Indian government introduced new uniform regulations that conflicted with the

Missionaries of Charity rules regarding placement of adopted children. These new rules required a much broader acceptance of the lifestyle of possible adoptive parents. Rather than violate their conscience and place children in homes they didn't think would be wholesome for the children's upbringing, the Missionaries of Charity suspended their adoption services in India, leaving adoption to other organizations in that country.

The Calcutta beginnings of the Missionaries of Charity were only the start. Mother Teresa wanted to expand out to the rest of the country. There was a rule in place, however, that a new religious order must remain within its home diocese for at least ten years before branching out. Archbishop Perier, ever cautious, insisted on the wisdom of the rule to protect from becoming overextended. Mother Teresa, therefore, waited until 1959 to expand within India outside of the Archdiocese of Calcutta. With Archbishop Perier's cautious permission, she then began opening outreaches in Delhi, Bombay (now Mumbai), and elsewhere. The spread of the Missionaries of Charity was swift throughout the country, with the start of new orphanages, dispensaries, and schools. A superior was placed in charge of each of the new convents to apply the rule of the order, maintain its spirituality, and report to Mother

Teresa as the superior general. From then on, Mother Teresa made frequent trips throughout India to visit the many centers of the Missionaries of Charity.

Mother Teresa was burning with the desire to quench the thirst of Jesus not only in India but throughout the world as well. Archbishop Perier insisted that expansion beyond India would be too much. But in 1965, the papal internuncio to New Delhi, Archbishop Knox, invited Mother Teresa to found an outreach in Venezuela. Given the proposal from the pope's own messenger, Archbishop Perier was made amenable to the new move. Mother Teresa sent five sisters for the new mission in Venezuela, where they filled a particular need there, answering the local priests' calls for providing religious education as part of their service to the poor.

Also in 1965, Pope Paul VI sent greetings and encouragement to the Missionaries of Charity and accepted their request to become a Society of Pontifical Right. This would enable them to carry out the mission worldwide. Invitations from various places appealed to Mother Teresa for help. The Missionaries of Charity were in Sri Lanka by 1967, Rome by 1968, and Caracas by 1970. In fact, Pope Paul VI personally asked

Mother Teresa in 1968, when she was at an audience with him, to send sisters to Rome to care for the poor.

According to Mother Teresa, the decision to found new centers is based on three criteria: the overflow of new vocations to the Missionaries of Charity, the invitation of the local bishop to serve the poor there, and finally an investigation by the Missionaries of Charity to determine the needs of the poor in the area (*No Greater Love*, 165).

# Persuasion by Authenticity

Journalists in India discovered Mother Teresa in the 1950s and made her work known throughout India. Donations poured in to the Missionaries of Charity as a result, fueling the order's growing needs. When Mother Teresa met Indian prime minister Jawaharlal Nehru for the first time, she began to tell him about the work of the Missionaries of Charity. He stopped her and said he already knew all about her work, and India was very grateful for it (Chawla, 78).

Mother Teresa came to the attention of television commentator Malcolm Muggeridge at the BBC in London. Muggeridge, an atheist, was a sharp critic of Christianity, known for pulling the threads out of perceived hypocrisy. An associate of his arranged for him to interview Mother Teresa. Muggeridge was interested in finding out what the Missionaries of Charity were really all about. His interviews thrived on controversy. Mother Teresa was warned about him but decided to make the trip to London anyway, convinced that good would come of it. Muggeridge was touched by her authenticity, and in the encounter with her, his eyes were opened to the many questions that troubled him about the meaning of life.

Muggeridge had spent time in Calcutta as a journalist and writes that he "found the place, even with all the comforts of a European's life ... barely tolerable" (*Something Beautiful for God*, 21). He was touched that she, of her own free will and after much patience waiting for her superiors' permission, "stepped out with a few rupees in her pocket, made her way to the poorest, wretchedest quarter of the city, found a lodging there, gathered together a few abandoned children ... and began her ministry of love" (19).

The arguments of Christianity held little sway to Muggeridge, who believed they simply served to cover ulterior motives. Mother Teresa was different. He wrote, "Mother Teresa moved in and stayed [in the slums of Calcutta].... She, a nun, rather slightly built ... not particularly clever, or particularly gifted in the arts of persuasion. Just with this Christian love shining about her; in her heart and on her lips. Just prepared to follow her Lord, and in accordance with his instructions regard every derelict left to die in the streets as him" (22). Muggeridge noted that while Christians seemed to be scrambling desperately to preserve the relevance of their religion in the changing culture, the answer was all there in this simple nun. She herself witnessed to the reality of Christianity by the authenticity of her love (31).

The interview was not of the best technical quality for broadcasting. Nonetheless, it made a strong impression on the audience. Many viewers sent in donations to be forwarded to the Missionaries of Charity to support their work. This was really the beginning of Western world's acquaintance with Mother Teresa.

Muggeridge decided to travel to Calcutta in 1969 to shoot a documentary on the work of the Missionaries of Charities. It was entitled *Something Beautiful for God*, the same title as the book he would later write on the subject. He was struck by Mother Teresa's intentional and loving oneness with the poor. He writes, "I never experienced so perfect a sense of human equality as with Mother Teresa among her poor. Her love for them, reflecting God's love, makes them equal, as brothers and sisters within a family are equal, however widely they differ in intellectual and other attainments, in physical beauty and grace" (23).

While filming the inside of Nirmal Hriday, the home of the dying, Muggeridge experienced what was to him, as a professional broadcaster, a miracle. The lighting conditions inside the dispensary were terrible for filming this important scene, showing those being cared for by the sisters, and Muggeridge and cameraman Ken MacMillan did not bring enough lighting to compensate. But when they watched the film later, it was as if the best lighting equipment had been brought in. It was suitable for broadcasting (*Something Beautiful for God*, 41).

Muggeridge was touched by Mother Teresa, and his interest in the spiritual was piqued, but his conversion took a long time as he struggled with the many difficulties he had with Catholicism and its history. Mother Teresa was so different from him. He writes, "Ecclesiastic authority ... is something that she accepts in the same unquestioning way that peasants accept the weather, or sailors storms at sea" (19). Mother Teresa walked with him in his questioning and prayed for him. She challenged him to put aside his doubts and make the leap of faith. Muggeridge was at last received into the Catholic Church in 1982 and became a spokesperson for belief to a culture that was losing faith.

# Making a Mark on the West

Mother Teresa was not always the public speaker she is remembered to be. Catholic Relief Services invited her to speak at their conference in 1960 in Las Vegas. She turned down the invitation, but they persisted. She left the matter to Archbishop Perier, who advised her to go to Las Vegas. It was a great penance for her, but was fruitful. On the way home, she made numerous stops around the world with an aim to founding new missions. Soon she was asked to speak the world over. She came to spend 80% of her time, in fact, outside of Calcutta, whether visiting homes she had established on every continent, requesting permission from government leaders to open new centers, or speaking the message of love and peace. This work, too, had to be done.

As a renowned journalist, Malcolm Muggeridge first nominated Mother Teresa for the Nobel Peace Prize in 1976, but she was passed over for several years. Some voters may have turned to other potential recipients because of Mother Teresa's religiosity and because they did not at first see the connection between her work of promoting human dignity and the cause for world peace in the sense of anti-violence. But more influential admirers, including Robert McNamara, president of the World Bank, and Edward Kennedy, joined in supporting her nomination; at last, she received the award in

1979 (Chawla, 185). Most of the world felt that it was she who graced the award, rather than the other way around.

Mother Teresa had received many awards already and would receive still more. The first medallion she had won in India she kept permanently around the neck of the statue of Mary at the Motherhouse, recognizing Our Lady as the one to be honored for the work. In 1983, Mother Teresa was received into the Order of Merit by Queen Elizabeth II. She also won the U.S. Presidential Medal of Freedom in 1985 and the Congressional Gold Medal in 1997. Mother Teresa's brother Lazar, the only member left of her immediate family, attended the ceremony for her Nobel Peace Prize. It was the first time they had seen each other since she had entered the religious life.

Mother Teresa decided to accept the Nobel Peace Prize on behalf of the poor and in order to make them and the work known to the world. Likewise, she accepted the prize money for the poor served by the Missionaries of Charity. Mother Teresa traveled to Oslo for the ceremony but requested that the usual stately dinner be cancelled and the money donated to the poor. It was important to her that those in attendance share in the suffering of the poor. She told them at the lecture,

"And I know well that you have not given from your abundance, but you have given until it has hurt you. Today the little children they have—I was so surprised—there is so much joy for the children that are hungry" (NobelPrize.org).

In her acceptance speech, Mother Teresa began with the Prayer of St. Francis, a prayer that all could be invited to pray: "Lord, make me a channel of Thy peace...." She spoke of the dignity of the human person, each created in God's image. Mother Teresa said even in the West, a great poverty is the lack of being loved, which is likewise at the root of poverty worldwide. She said, "And so here I am talking with you—I want you to find the poor here, right in your own home first. And begin love there. Be that good news to your own people. And find out about your next-door neighbor." Respect for the dignity of each person is the foundation for peace. Mother Teresa took the opportunity to point out the culture's vulnerability to a mentality of violence by abortion—the killing of the unwanted child. She told those gathered, "And this is what is the greatest destroyer of peace today. Because if a mother can kill her own child—what is left for me to kill you and you kill me—there is nothing between."

Mother Teresa made use of her renown to further her work for peace. Conflict broke out in the Middle East with the Siege of Beirut. None of the world leaders were able to so much as work out a ceasefire between Israel and Lebanon. The only one who could do it, respected by all, was Mother Teresa. Working from Rome in collaboration with Pope John Paul II, she pleaded for a ceasefire so she could personally go to Beirut and rescue three dozen handicapped children who were displaced when their hospital was damaged by fighter jets. She got exactly what she asked for and saved those frightened children before hostilities broke out again. The *New York Times* reported, "Her wrinkled face broke into a broad grin as she entered the Dar al-Ajaza al-Islamia Mental Hospital and began embracing the children, huddled in a group on the floor.... Most of the children seemed unaware of what was happening. Some began to cry. The nun tried to comfort them" (Aug. 15, 1982).

In 1984, poisonous gas escaped from a Union Carbide plant at Bhopal in central India. Residents were sleeping in their beds when they began inhaling the toxic fumes from the methyl isocyanate that had been released. Thousands died and hundreds of thousands were harmed. According to the BBC, one survivor told reporters, "Mothers didn't know their children had died, children didn't know their mothers had died and men didn't know their whole families had died." (Dec. 3, 1984). Mother Teresa and seven sisters went to Bhopal a few days after the accident to provide what comfort they could. The *New York Times* reported, "At the hospitals, doctors, nurses and policemen pushed back crowds to create a passage for her. At the Government's Hamidia Hospital, she asked her fellow sisters of the Missionaries of Charity order to write down the names of orphans and seriously ill children .... She touched the survivors on their arms and hands, kissed children, patted their heads and lingered over malnourished infants who were having difficulty breathing" (Dec. 12, 1984).

Mother Teresa told reporters, "It is terrible suffering, nothing like this has happened before .... One beautiful thing. It has brought out the best in everybody.... This has got those people to share, to serve the suffering who would never have become involved otherwise" (*New York Times*). She also urged forgiveness for those responsible in the aftermath of the disaster. Bhopal was a singularly frightening tragedy, but often when Mother Teresa encountered great suffering, she would sadly and tenderly say, "Never have I seen such suffering." She understood that each instance of suffering is unique; it is not measured on a scale.

Mother Teresa's presence drew attention to situations that the West would have ignored otherwise. If there was a famine, she was there. Mother Teresa also became a trusted friend to many world leaders, to whom she came often in order to request permission to open new centers to serve the poor. She was also able to direct their attention to situations that needed their assistance. After much effort, she even convinced Soviet premiere Mikhail Gorbechev to allow her to open the first new religious outreaches in the Soviet Union since 1918. When at first she got no reply, she sent him a telegraph wishing him a happy St. Michael's Day (Chawla, 79). Mother Teresa also had a good relationship with Princess Diana of the U. K. and U. S. President Ronald Reagan, who readily appropriated funds she requested for a famine in Ethiopia.

Mother Teresa was one of the first to provide care for a new kind of 'leprosy' in the West—namely, AIDS. Responding urgently to the need, she set up an AIDS clinic in 1985 in New York's Greenwich Village before the government even took notice of the new disease. The Missionaries of Charity found much work among the unwanted in urban centers in the United States. In fact, the order has more centers in the U. S. than in any country other than India.

Mother Teresa was particularly close with Pope Saint John Paul II. Likewise of Slavic ancestry, he appreciated her unswerving fidelity to Church teaching and her unique authentic spirituality. He even entrusted her with serving as a messenger for him numerous times to world leaders and in difficult situations. Mother Teresa had great respect for John Paul II, and he for her. Pope John Paul II was a visitor at Nirmal Hriday in 1986. She told reporters that it "was the happiest day of my life" (BBC, Feb. 3, 1986). According to the BBC, "When the pontiff arrived at the two-storey building in the heart of the city's slums, Mother Teresa climbed into the famous white Popemobile and bent down to kiss his hand. He kissed the top of her head and she took him into the home she founded in 1950 called Nirmal Hriday, or Sacred Heart.... During his half-hour visit, the Pope who was visibly moved by what he saw, helped the nuns to feed the sick and dying. He gave plates of food to those strong enough to feed themselves and handed out more plates to the nuns to spoon-feed the weakest."

Mother Teresa asked John Paul II to open a Missionaries of Charity outreach center in the Vatican itself. John Paul II's biographer George Weigel writes, "The managers of popes had said that this was impossible. How could you introduce the poor and vagrants into the Vatican? What about security? John Paul II kept pressing and a solution was finally found—to take over and renovate a building on the edge of the Vatican City State, beside the Congregation for the Doctrine of the Faith but still within the Vatican walls" (*Witness to Hope*, 566). In fact, before Mother Teresa could come back and remind the Pope of what she wanted, as he knew she would, he found a way to honor her request despite the limited space available. The Casa Dono di Maria ('Gift of Mary' House) opened in 1988, providing meals and lodging for the homeless within the Vatican itself, and remains there to this day.

The Pope even based his 1993 Lenten message to the world on her spirituality of the dying Christ's thirst for souls. John Paul II wrote, "Look upon Jesus nailed to the Cross, dying, and listen to his faint voice: 'I thirst.' Today, Christ repeats his request and relives the torments of his Passion in the poorest of our brothers and sisters" (Sept. 18, 1992, Vatican.va). Mother Teresa took consolation from the Holy Father's words that what she was doing was indeed fulfilling Christ's desire.

# The Pain of Longing

For Mother Teresa, the most important aspect of her life was her spirituality, and that is precisely where she suffered the most. The success of her order brought her little consolation. From her first days on the streets of Calcutta, Mother Teresa experienced an intense loneliness. Experiencing the loneliness and misery of the poor, she felt that God was not with her. This feeling did not go away even when she was joined by many sisters.

The world, and even the sisters, only came to know about this when her private letters were released after her death during her beatification process. Father Brian Kolodiejchuk, a Canadian-born priest of the Missionaries of Charity and a spiritual director to Mother Teresa towards the end of her life, was entrusted with presenting her cause to the Vatican. During this process, he compiled five volumes on Mother Teresa and her writings, from which he published a collection of her private letters and notes, with commentary, in his 2007 book *Come Be My Light: The Private Writings of the 'Saint' of Calcutta*. The 2014 movie on Mother Teresa entitled *The Letters* was based on the new revelations from that book, from which the world first learned about her locutions from God, her secret vow to deny God nothing, and her five decades of interior darkness. Some, not understanding the spiritual world and thought of Mother Teresa, thought that it meant that Mother Teresa was really an atheist and therefore a hypocrite.

Many people have an empty spot in their heart, which they don't know God can fill and which they cover over with many distractions. For Mother Teresa, the emptiness was not an ordinary restlessness but a positive, searing pain. She had experienced the bliss of close spiritual union with God as few do. She had spoken intimately to God, her spouse, and she heard him speaking clearly and tenderly to her. God had filled her soul with a joy beyond compare. He had given her clarity in her mission. She understood what he wanted of her, and the thought of being simply a "pencil his His hand" was a great consolation to her. Her greatest joy was simply to sit for hours in God's presence, especially in Eucharistic Adoration, and exchange glances of love. This consolation came to end as she answered God's "call within a call."

Her whole life revolved around the things of God, yet when she thought of them, she drew a blank. As she experienced the suffering of the world, it did not make sense to her that God even existed. When she prayed or looked for guidance, there was simply the void. When she thought on her soul, it seemed like a fiction. When she tried to contemplate Heaven, the reward of faithfulness, she saw simply nothingness. As for the pains of hell, she wrote that she could understand that. It was especially the searing pain of emptiness and separation from the One the soul is made for. Her namesake, St. Therese of Lisieux, wrote of similar feelings. She was likewise focused solely on the things of God but experienced this intense absence towards the end of her young life.

Mother Teresa wrote that at certain points she did not "believe" in God, but not in the sense of an atheist. According to St. Thomas Aquinas, the assent of faith is "an act of the intellect as determined to one object by the will" (*Summa Theologica* II–II, 2, 1, ad. 3 [NewAdvent.org]). In other words, while the intellect must focus on an object (ie., the existence of God), the will must move it into focus by free choice. She chose to believe and to accept God's gift of faith even though it was not clear to her. To Mother Teresa, the existence of God was a given whether or not she could experience it within herself. She wrote to a spiritual director, "I call, I cling, I want—and there is no One to answer—no One on whom I can cling—no, No One.—Alone" (*Come Be My Light*, 187). She spoke even of the absence of God in divine terms, taking the objectivity of God's existence as a given despite her subjective feelings about it. Objections arose in her mind, but she wrote that she would not repeat them so as not to offend God.

Another aspect of the pain for Mother Teresa was her intense longing for God, which seemed unfulfilled. In her revelations, Jesus had shown how bitterly he longs for souls. Mother Teresa asked for such a longing for God and souls in return, and that is what she received. But the object of that longing was denied her. Where others would have given up and taken their life in a different direction, Mother Teresa kept the course, driven largely by the vow she had made to deny nothing that God asked. She was so faithful to that vow that she said she wrote she would rather die than violate it (*Come Be My Light*, 32). She was tempted many times to say no to what she thought God wanted of her, and these were times of crisis to her. Nonetheless, she stayed heroically true to her vow.

# At Peace with the Darkness

What Mother Teresa at first called "the dark night of the birth of the Society" became simply a way of life. The feeling of emptiness in her relationship with God extended also to that with her trusted spiritual director, Father Van Exem (*Come Be My Light*, 164). She continued to confess to him for a number of years and to seek his advice occasionally on matters relating to the order, but as time went on, she could not bring herself to speak of the continued darkness. Archbishop Perier, meanwhile, was not simply an administrative hurdle for Mother Teresa to overcome in establishing the order, or simply as the superior to which she must defer; rather she saw him as a true father whose advice she regarded as divine guidance. Corresponding by letter, he offered her much comfort during the first decade of her darkness. He spoke of periods of the 'dark night of the soul' experienced by most of the saints as a purification for reaching greater holiness. He spoke of offering up sufferings and trusting in God's promises and love.

Mother Teresa was extremely guarded in sharing her spiritual secrets with anyone, but felt called to be open about them to a retreat master named Father Lawrence Picachy in 1956, who then became her spiritual director before being transferred to a new assignment in 1960. During this time, Mother Teresa was able to sense a hint of God's presence in the faces of the poor. She saw their suffering as the suffering of Christ, and she offered her own sufferings to alleviate theirs. Somehow, she thought, perhaps God could make use of the darkness. If there was any use for it in God's eyes, she was willing to undergo it, even forever if need be.

In April of 1958, Mother Teresa received a special grace at Archbishop Perier's requiem Mass for Pope Pius XII, who had recently passed. She had prayed that she would be given at least a short period of time in which she could again experience God's light and love. She was granted that grace, which meant so much to her, and it remained with her for about a month. Everything made sense to her and she felt radiating with the love of God. She would never again experience this in her lifetime. Other people said they saw God's love radiating through her, but she herself could not sense it. Typically, it was only through the remembrance of past events that she could know the love of God in her life. That is why anniversaries were so important to her— anniversaries of her inspiration, of her profession in religious life, and so forth.

Father Brian Kolodiejchuk notes that despite offering much-needed comfort to Mother Teresa, neither Archbishop Perier nor Father Picachy, a future bishop, fully understood the roots of Mother Teresa's darkness, which was so very unusual even among the saints. At last Mother Teresa found the answer to the meaning of her interior suffering from a Jesuit priest named Father Joseph Neuner, who had written an article about the work of the Missionaries of Charity in 1957. She reached out to him and later invited him to preach a retreat for the sisters in 1961. Mother Teresa revealed her spiritual secrets to him, and his answer gave her the peace she was looking for.

Father Neuner said that this extended period of darkness was not the usual dark night of the soul by which God purifies the soul. Rather, the darkness itself was the very manner of God's unity with her. The longing for God within her was an indication of the presence of God (*Come Be My Light*, 214). The darkness was given to her by God as an experience of his thirst for souls and of the emptiness of the poor in their need for God. Through the darkness, her "calling within a call" was interiorized. This knowledge gave Mother Teresa a peace and resignation within a darkness that would never again abate. She came to cling to the darkness as the presence of God in her life. When people would share about their own sufferings with Mother Teresa, she would encourage them to offer it to God. She did not promise that this would bring feelings of happiness. Rather, it would unite them with the sufferings of Christ. That was her experience.

Still, Mother Teresa was remembered as a very joyful person, even exuding joy. She smiled often, for happiness as a feeling is not the same as joy. According to St. Thomas Aquinas, "spiritual joy, which is about God, is caused by charity" (*Summa Theologica* II–II, 28, 1). Even in the midst of sorrow of one kind, joy was still possible for Mother Teresa. St. Thomas further writes, "There can be spiritual joy about God in two ways. First, when we rejoice in the Divine good considered in itself; secondly, when we rejoice in the Divine good as participated by us" (*Summa Theologica* II–II, 28, 1, ad. 3). It seems Mother Teresa experienced some of the first, especially in her encounters with the poor, while rarely experiencing the second. For Mother Teresa, in God and in service, there is always cause for joy, even in the midst of pain. There is always a reason for a smile. Still, Mother Teresa wrote that it was often hard for her to smile at Jesus; he was a very difficult spouse.

# Mother Teresa's Message

Mother Teresa was not known for her eloquence but for her sincerity. Though she often repeated similar phrases, they echoed a practical but deep-lived wisdom inspired by traditional Catholic spirituality. Numerous inspirational books compile the many writings, speeches, and thoughts of Mother Teresa, which have been read by peoples of various faiths and walks of life. They saw her as a credible voice, radically putting her message into practice rather than only talking. While she did not actively preach to make converts for Catholicism in her work among the poor, she clearly saw the world from the perspective of Catholic faith. Everyone is created in the image of God, is loved by God, and is made for heaven. Mother Teresa saw Jesus in everyone, and she prayed that they would be attracted to the truth that she had received.

Mother Teresa challenges everyone to allow time in their lives for quiet so they can encounter God. She wrote, "In the silence of the heart God speaks. If you face God in prayer and silence, God will speak to you" (*No Greater Love,* 7). Prayer, for her and in the tradition of St. Therese of Lisieux, is a glance towards heaven. Mother Teresa writes: "Often a deep and fervent look at Christ is the best prayer: I look at Him and He looks at me. When you come face to face with God, you cannot but know that you are nothing, that you have nothing" (*No Greater Love*, 6). While some place more emphasis on service than on prayer, Mother Teresa insists that it is precisely prayer that enables one to love.

Mother Teresa encouraged people to live simply and to suffer in solidarity with the poor. It is one thing to give, but it is another to give until it hurts—even just to go without something small now and then and give the money to the poor. The poor do not choose poverty. Their poverty is the result of the lack of love on behalf of other people. Still, many of the poor do not know how to make use of their poverty. But those who choose poverty can find spiritual freedom in it. Out of the little they have, some choose to give to others even less fortunate than themselves. They are not weighed down by the cares of the world. Mother Teresa and her sisters chose to become poor so that they could serve the poor. She wrote, "Poverty is necessary because we are working with the poor. When they complain about the food, we can say, we eat the same.... We have to go down and lift them up. It opens the heart of the poor when we can say we live the same way they do" (*No Greater Love*, 98). In this way, Mother Teresa imitated the love of Christ, who despite being God, became human to raise us up.

Every year to this day, thousands of young people visit the Missionaries of Charity to share in their work for at least a short period of time. Some make a further step to begin the long process of becoming a sister or brother while others go home with a heart more opened to God and the poor. Many are not Catholic or Christian. David Jolly, a reporter for the *New York Times,* writes of his experience of volunteering with the Missionaries of Charity in Calcutta: "Going to help out with the Missionaries of Charity might sound daunting, but nothing could be more simple. I showed up at Kolkata's Netaji Subhash Airport after 10 p.m. with no hotel reservation, not knowing anyone. A taxi got me to Sudder Street, where I found a hotel—it won't show up in any luxury travel guides—and learned everything I needed to know about volunteering by asking" (Oct. 27, 2007). He writes of his volunteerism at Nirmal Hriday, "Instead of the solemn, oppressive atmosphere I have been anticipating, I find a beehive of activity and, once again, a lively sense of camaraderie among the volunteers. The sisters come from all over the world, including India, and they are kind and extremely efficient.... When a no-nonsense Italian nurse puts me to work feeding little pots of what I imagine to be banana custard to a sightless and nearly toothless old man, I jump at the chance to be useful."

But Mother Teresa did not ask everyone to come to Calcutta to join her. She challenged everyone to find their own Calcutta at home—first in their own family and then in the poor of their own area. It's harder at first simply to live in peace and love with one's own family, and therefore we are often blind to the less fortunate around us. If everyone would do just that, the world would be a much better place. Yet Mother Teresa wasn't focused on changing the whole world; she saw her work as just a drop in the ocean. She was committed to faithfulness, not success, but she saw herself as an instrument God chose to use. Everyone could open themselves to such an attitude—to such a life.

In particular, Mother Teresa encouraged a culture that was open to life and welcomed children. She encouraged spending time with one's children and tending to them as gifts from God. She encouraged the use of Natural Family Planning as way to regulate births as opposed to artificial contraception, which is closed to the possibility of new life. She strongly decried abortion, saying that it not only snuffs out the lives of innocents but also introduces great guilt into the lives of all involved terminating the pregnancy. When people said a celibate nun didn't have anything to say on the matter, she pointed to the sacrifices she made to provide happy homes for children and to care for the needs of women.

For Mother Teresa, abortion was a great spiritual poverty in the West, but certainly not the only one. She wrote, "The world today is hungry not only for bread but hungry for love, hungry to be wanted, to be loved. They're hungry to feel the presence of Christ.... In every country there are poor. On certain continents poverty is more spiritual than material, a poverty that consists of loneliness, discouragement, and the lack of meaning in life" (*No Greater Love*, 93).

# Opposition

Not everyone was open to Mother Teresa's message or approving of her works. Even during her canonization, major news outlets pushed stories recalling her critics' scathing attacks. Mother Teresa's most noted critic was atheist commentator Christopher Hitchens, who came out with a documentary called *Hell's Angel* in 1994 and a book *The Missionary Position: Mother Teresa in Theory and Practice* in 1995, both of which made the case against her. In an act of iconoclasm, Hitchens left aside the aura of goodness and holiness surrounding the figure of Mother Teresa and analyzed her actions and practices from a purely materialistic point of view that also assumed the hypocrisy of Catholicism and Christianity in general.

Hitchens, who as a secular humanist had an interest in eliminating world poverty, came to volunteer with the Missionaries of Charity and was given a tour by Mother Teresa herself. Whereas the formerly atheist Malcolm Muggeridge gradually had all his questions answered through his encounters with Mother Teresa, it was not so for Hitchens. Hitchens was turned off immediately by several things: by people kissing Mother Teresa's feet as a sign of reverence, by a sign at the entrance of the dispensary (taken from Proverbs 12:1 in the Bible) that read "He that loveth correction loveth knowledge," and by a comment by Mother Teresa that her works served to combat abortion and contraception in Calcutta (*The Missionary Position*, 23–24). Hitchens collected criticisms of the Missionaries of Charities from healthcare professionals and news stories showing her accepting donations from dictators and corrupt businessmen to make the case that Mother Teresa was not altruistic but had ulterior and even sinister motives for doing what she did.

Hitchens cited critiques from visiting medical professionals that Missionaries of Charity dispensaries for the dying in India were substandard. They point out a lack of modern medical equipment and modern medical screening practices and tests which could otherwise save lives. They observe that painkillers were not used and syringes were reused many times, run under cold water but not properly sterilized (Hitchens, 37–41). Hitchens pointed to the large donations pouring into the Missionaries of Charity and argued that the money could have been better used funding a few state-of-the-art facilities in Calcutta rather than spread thin the world-over.

Hitchens alleged that Mother Teresa actually wanted to preserve abject poverty, like what we hear about in Calcutta, diverting attention from the need for real social change and the elimination of poverty. He said that overall, modern-day Kolkata really wasn't that bad, but Mother Teresa focused on the worst because it suited her aims. For Hitchens, Mother Teresa, a duly-honored foot soldier for the powers that be, wallowed in the misery of the poor simply to soothe the consciences of the rich in the West, who despite the oppression they caused, could be satisfied that at least someone was doing for the poor what they were not (15).

Christopher Hitchens had his chance to persuade even the Vatican of his theories on Mother Teresa, testifying against her during the canonization process (Greene, 137). In the end, of course, Mother Teresa was canonized. The Vatican rejected many of his criticisms, recognizing them as foreign to the mindset of the actual Mother Teresa and belying a general anti-religious bias. They further regarded the plausible criticisms as not precluding heroic virtue in Mother Teresa. To be a saint, one does not have to be humanly or professionally perfect, but one must demonstrate the theological virtues of faith, hope, and charity and the cardinal virtues of prudence, temperance, fortitude, and justice to a heroic degree.

The criticisms of Mother Teresa's dispensaries were based on standards in the West rather than in India. Also, her dispensaries were for those who could not be admitted to hospitals, and they were brought there mostly from the streets because they were dying. The purpose was indeed to give them love and dignity during the natural process of dying. Indeed, aside from basic medicine and nutrition, they were generally not given treatments to prolong life nor to induce death. Her dispensaries were not themselves hospitals.

Maintaining strict poverty has been a theme of many Catholic religious orders for centuries. The equality of Mother Teresa's dispensaries consisted of the poor essentially being cared for by other poor. Hence, Mother Teresa intentionally avoided expensive modern medical equipment, to maintain this equal poverty. Mother Teresa was sparse in the use of painkillers because she believed in the spiritual value of pain and taught this to those suffering. Though not typically applied this way, this is rooted in the Catholic belief in redemptive suffering.

It is true that Mother Teresa's intention was not the elimination of world poverty. Her focus, based on the call of Christ, was to tend primarily to the person at hand, in which she saw the image of God. She sent her missionaries around the world to witnesses to Christ's light and love. She saw giving to the poor as an opportunity for rich people, even iniquitous ones, for taking a step towards doing what's right.

The name of her order indeed includes the word 'missionary,' but she was not about proselytizing or about colonization with Western ideas. She believed wholly in the Catholic faith and preached by example and by the witness of who she was. She was respectful of Hinduism and other religions, even recognizing that people may be able to find light from God there. The Missionaries of Charity, as a pointedly Indian order, were actually a development in step with the needs of India's independence and in keeping with Indian culture. Mother Teresa is overall very highly honored and respected in India to this day, and has been recognized by the government with numerous awards and honors. The Indian government even printed a postage stamp in her honor. Mother Teresa was aware of poverty everywhere and not only in India, founding missions in cities such as New York and Washington.

The Vatican concluded that Mother Teresa's intentions were right in accepting donations from dictators, providing them with an opportunity to choose goodness (Greene, 137–138). They also concluded that Mother Teresa was not required to try to eliminate world poverty but only to tend to the poor before her as individuals. While others might stand up to dictators or directly combat the underlying causes of poverty, this was not Mother Teresa's way or mission.

Mother Teresa was warned from the beginning about the difficulties and possible failures of the work she desired to take on. Staying within the cloister would have been much safer not only for her health but also for her reputation. Still, she went out into the streets as a simple Christian woman, very much in the minority and very much with the odds against her; she made herself vulnerable despite the likeliness of misunderstanding from all sides. Hitchens's book and documentary were both released just a few years before Mother Teresa's death. She did not watch or read any of it, but was told about it by the sisters. She said she forgave Hitchens. Hitchens, upon hearing of this, took offense because he had never asked for forgiveness (88).

In life, Mother Teresa was much grieved at the thought of not pleasing Jesus. The criticisms in Hitchens's book and documentary, however, seemed not to bother her very much. She dealt with them much the same way that she dealt with praise. Once, when asked how she handled her celebrity, she said, "Jesus has given me a very great grace and that is: the deepest conviction of my total nothingness. If He could find a poorer woman through whom to do his work, He would not choose me, but He would choose that woman ... it goes in here [pointing to her ears] and it comes out there; it goes right through me" (*Come Be My Light*, 294).

# Eternal Reward

Even in her old age, Mother Teresa kept up her fast-paced schedule, caring for the sick, visiting Missionaries of Charity homes, and traveling the world as a messenger of peace. The only rule of the order she exempted herself from was traveling with another sister. She said she would probably wear them out. Mother Teresa worked hard during her old age to develop and grow the Missionary Brothers of Charity. She also worked for peace in the Middle East when the Gulf War was brewing.

As she grew older, her toes became more gnarled from many years of sacrifices she had made. When footwear was donated, she gave the best to the poor and kept only the worst sandals for herself.

To the very end of her life, the darkness persisted. Her understanding of it, however, grew. She had the presence of God and bore its fruits to others despite not being able to experience it herself. God sent her a sign, though, that he was with her. While she was visiting in Rome in 1987, a priest she did not know came with a simple message for her that he believed was from God: "Tell Mother Teresa, I thirst" (*Come Be My Light*, 310). That was all.

At the age of 72, Mother Teresa had her first heart attack, falling out of her bed one night while visiting in Rome. The United Press reported on June 10, 1983, "Mother Teresa of Calcutta is undergoing treatment for poor blood circulation and refusing pain killers so she can offer her suffering to God, her doctor said Friday. 'She never stopped to take care of herself,' Dr. Vincenzo Bilotta of Rome's Salvador Mundi hospital said. 'Finally she decided to stop and take care of herself.'" Mother Teresa's health problems continued. She received a pacemaker after her second heart attack in 1989. While visiting in Mexico in 1991, she came down with pneumonia, which led to yet another heart attack. Her immune system weakened; she even contracted malaria in 1996, and also suffered from multiple falls.

Mother Teresa was in critical condition in the hospital just ahead of her planned trip to China to try to introduce the Missionaries of Charity to that country. Father Van Exem, now age 84, was likewise in critical condition at that time. He shared his prayer intentions with Mother Teresa by way of letter: "...that you may have no operation, that you may be in China by the 7th October 93, that the Lord may take me and not you if that is His Will" (*Come Be My Light*, 322). Father Van

Exem died four days later, and Mother Teresa recovered and was able to make her trip.

Mother Teresa thought many times about stepping down as superior general of the Missionaries of Charity. She urged the sisters to elect someone else at their 1985 general meeting, but they chose her again. In 1991, Mother Teresa informed Pope John Paul II of her intentions to resign, but finding a suitable replacement was a challenge. Mother Teresa said the Missionaries of Charity needed someone so small that they would allow God to really run the Society. But no one 'smaller' than her could easily be found.

Mother Teresa was again in critical condition by late 1996, suffering with many tubes and wires. A Tabernacle with the Eucharist was placed in her room. A Hindu doctor told one of the priests that Mother Teresa was constantly looking at that box, and that it seems to make her feel better (*Come Be My Light*, 328).

At last, crippled by infirmity, Mother Teresa announced her resignation in January of 1997, just a few months before her death. Settling on a replacement was still the challenge. To overcome their indecision, the sisters submitted to John Paul

II. The Pope decided that Mother Teresa should remain the titular head of the order but that Sister Mary Nirmala, an Indian and a convert from Hinduism, would take over as superior general (Greene, 115). To maintain a sense of equality with the sisters, Sister Nirmala chose to retain the title of 'Sister' rather than 'Mother.' Mother Teresa continued to be very much part of running the society, and Sister Nirmala accommodated for her.

When her health improved somewhat, Mother Teresa made one last trip around the world to spread her message, taking breaks as needed to regain her strength. One of the people she met with was Princess Diana, who would die in a car crash just days before Mother Teresa's own passing later that year. In June, together they visited the poor in the Bronx in New York City. According to the *National Catholic Reporter*, Mother Teresa sent these words of condolence in early September to the family of the Princess of Wales: "She was very concerned for the poor. She was very anxious to do something for them, and it was beautiful. That is why she was close to me."

At the Motherhouse at Calcutta on the evening of September 5, 1997, Mother Teresa complained of severe back pain and had difficulty breathing. She needed the help of a breathing machine. Medical professionals arrived promptly, but the power went out and the backup generator failed to start. It was Mother Teresa's time. She was 87 years old. Her work and her suffering were over. Her reward was at hand. As Jesus said, "Then the king will say to those on his right, 'Come, you who are blessed by my Father. Inherit the kingdom prepared for you from the foundation of the world. For I was hungry and you gave me food, I was thirsty and you gave me drink, a stranger and you welcomed me, naked and you clothed me, ill and you cared for me, in prison and you visited me.... Amen, I say to you, whatever you did for one of these least brothers of mine, you did for me'" (Matthew 25:34–16, 40).

Mother Teresa's eternal reward was not because of her success, yet success followed from her commitment to the work and God's providence. According to Rome Reports, at the time of her death there were 3,914 Missionaries of Charity sisters and 363 brothers working in 120 countries around the word, operating some 594 centers. While religious vocations in general have declined in recent years, vocations to the Missionaries of Charity continue to grow, even after Mother Teresa's passing. In 2016, there were 5,161 sisters and 416 brothers operating 758 houses in 139 countries. At the time of Mother Teresa's passing, there were also about one million coworkers committed to sharing in the work through their daily lives.

Mother Teresa's body was laid for open viewing within a glass enclosure at St. Thomas Church for a whole week as thousands filed passed to pay her their respects. Indian Prime Minister Inder Kumar Gujral was likewise in attendance to honor Mother Teresa. He told reporters, "We had Gandhi in the first half of the century to show us the path to fight against poverty, and in the second half we have the Mother to show us the path to work for the poor.... She is no more. Millions are feeling that they have become orphaned. I am one of the orphans" (CNN, Sept. 7, 1997). On September 13, because of the large crowds, her funeral Mass had to be held in a large stadium, presided over by the highest clergy and attended by world leaders and their representatives as well as throngs of the poor. Mother Teresa's casket, draped with the Indian flag, was processed in state through the streets by Indian soldiers to the sound of bagpipes to its final resting place just outside the Motherhouse. Her body was borne on the same gun carriage that had carried the bodies of Mahatma Gandhi and Jawaharlal Nehru many years before (Greene, 137).

Very shortly after Mother Teresa's passing, Father Brian Kolodiejchuk, who would compile some 35,000 pages on her life and spirituality, was entrusted by the Archdiocese of Calcutta with investigating her life with a view to beatification. In 1999, Pope John Paul II gave special dispensation for the official process of Mother Teresa's beatification to begin, prior to the usual five years of waiting. In 2002, following the opinion of doctors on a lack of medical explanation, the Vatican approved Mother Teresa's first posthumous miracle—the disappearance of an abdominal tumor of an Indian Hindu woman. The woman's husband had placed an image of Mother Teresa, given him by the Missionaries of Charity, on her abdomen, and saw light coming from it. Pope John Paul II beatified Mother Teresa in St. Peter's Square on October 19, 2003.

In 2015, the Vatican approved a second miracle attributed to Mother Teresa. A Brazilian man was inexplicably healed of brain tumors after calling on Mother Teresa's intercession. On September 4, 2016, on the eve of the nineteenth anniversary of her passing, Pope Francis solemnly proclaimed Mother Teresa a saint before tens of thousands gathered at St. Peter's Square. The Knights of Columbus commissioned American artist Chas Fagan to produce a painting of Mother Teresa to be hung from the façade of St. Peter's for the occasion. The painting portrays Mother Teresa, with a slight halo around her head, smiling joyfully at a person in front of her, out of view from the painting (*New Haven Register*, Sept. 3, 2016). Pope Francis quipped in his closing remarks that it will be hard to call her St. Teresa of Calcutta, observing that "her sanctity is so close to us, so tender and fruitful, that spontaneously we will continue to call her 'Mother Teresa'" (Catholic News Service, Sept. 4, 2016).

# Conclusion

Mother Teresa was a witness to love. For her, love was the answer, but she did not simply tell us we must love. By unfailing example, she showed us what it means to love one's neighbor with God's love. Mother Teresa brought love where there was none and where people had forgotten how to love. For her, it was not about the outcome so much as about the person. It was about treating them like the unique and unrepeatable creation of God that they are.

Mother Teresa showed that sanctity of the most heroic kind is still possible in modern times. She also gives us consolation that sometimes not even saints walk their path with clarity; sometimes they too have to cling blindly to their faith.

Mother Teresa, the Saint of Calcutta, was very much in the midst of the world and of the daily concerns of some of its most vulnerable members, but as one who brought Christ to them and whose interior life was truly centered on Christ. Thus, the praise and also the bitterness of the world meant nothing to her in comparison to the words of Jesus: "Well done, my good and faithful servant…. Come, share your master's joy" (Matthew 25:23).

## About the Author

Michael J. Ruszala is the author of several religious books and holds an M.A. in Theology & Christian Ministry and a B.A. in Philosophy and Theology *summa cum laude* from Franciscan University of Steubenville. He is a Catholic lay ministry professional and has served as a parish lifelong faith formation director, a parish music director, and as an adjunct lecturer in religious studies at Niagara University in Lewiston, NY. Certified in parish catechetical leadership by the Diocese of Buffalo, he is the recipient of the 2016 Christian Service Award from the Canisius College Sodality of Our Lady. Please visit www.michaeljruszala.com for more information.

*Please enjoy the first two chapters of Pope Francis: Pastor of Mercy, written by Michael J. Ruszala, as available from Wyatt North Publishing.*

# Pope Francis: Pastor of Mercy

## Chapter 1

There is something about Pope Francis that captivates and delights people, even people who hardly know anything about him. He was elected in only two days of the conclave, yet many who tried their hand at speculating on who the next pope might be barely included him on their lists. The evening of Wednesday, March 13, 2013, the traditional white smoke poured out from the chimney of the Sistine Chapel and spread throughout the world by way of television, Internet, radio, and social media, signaling the beginning of a new papacy.

As the light of day waned from the Eternal City, some 150,000 people gathered watching intently for any movement behind the curtained door to the loggia of St. Peter's. A little after 8:00 p.m., the doors swung open and Cardinal Tauran emerged to pronounce the traditional and joyous Latin formula to introduce the new Bishop of Rome: "Annuncio vobis gaudium magnum; habemus papam!" ("I announce to you a great joy: we have a pope!") He then announced the new Holy Father's identity: "Cardinalem Bergoglio..."

The name Bergoglio, stirred up confusion among most of the faithful who flooded the square that were even more clueless than the television announcers were, who scrambled to figure out who exactly the new pope was. Pausing briefly, Cardinal

Tauran continued by announcing the name of the new pope: "...qui sibi nomen imposuit Franciscum" ("who takes for himself the name Francis"). Whoever this man may be, his name choice resonated with all, and the crowd erupted with jubilant cheers. A few moments passed before the television announcers and their support teams informed their global audiences that the man who was about to walk onto the loggia dressed in white was Cardinal Jorge Mario Bergoglio, age 76, of Buenos Aires, Argentina.

To add to the bewilderment and kindling curiosity, when the new pope stepped out to the thunderous applause of the crowd in St. Peter's Square, he did not give the expected papal gesture of outstretched arms. Instead, he gave only a simple and modest wave. Also, before giving his first apostolic blessing, he bowed asking the faithful, from the least to the greatest, to silently pray for him. These acts were only the beginning of many more words and gestures, such as taking a seat on the bus with the cardinals, refusing a popemobile with bulletproof glass, and paying his own hotel bill after his election, that would raise eyebrows among some familiar with papal customs and delight the masses.

Is he making a pointed critique of previous pontificates? Is he simply posturing a persona to the world at large to make a point? The study of the life of Jorge Mario Bergoglio gives a clear answer, and the answer is no. This is simply who he is as a man and as a priest. The example of his thought- provoking gestures flows from his character, his life experiences, his religious vocation, and his spirituality. This book uncovers the life of the 266th Bishop of Rome, Jorge Mario Bergoglio, also known as Father Jorge, a name he preferred even while he was an archbishop and cardinal.

What exactly do people find so attractive about Pope Francis? Aldo Cagnoli, a layman who developed a friendship with the Pope when he was serving as a cardinal, shares the following: "The greatness of the man, in my humble opinion lies not in building walls or seeking refuge behind his wisdom and office, but rather in dealing with everyone judiciously, respectfully, and with humility, being willing to learn at any moment of life; that is what Father Bergoglio means to me" (as quoted in Ch. 12 of Pope Francis: Conversations with Jorge Bergoglio, previously published as El Jesuita [The Jesuit]).

At World Youth Day 2013, in Rio de Janeiro, Brazil, three million young people came out to celebrate their faith with

Pope Francis. Doug Barry, from EWTN's Life on the Rock, interviewed youth at the event on what features stood out to them about Pope Francis. The young people seemed most touched by his authenticity. One young woman from St. Louis said, "He really knows his audience. He doesn't just say things to say things... And he is really sincere and genuine in all that he does." A friend agreed: "He was looking out into the crowd and it felt like he was looking at each one of us...." A young man from Canada weighed in: "You can actually relate to [him]... for example, last night he was talking about the World Cup and athletes." A young woman added, "I feel he means what he says... he practices what he preaches... he states that he's there for the poor and he actually means it."

The Holy Spirit guided the College of Cardinals in its election of Pope Francis to meet the needs of the Church following the historic resignation of Pope Benedict XVI due to old age. Representing the growth and demographic shift in the Church throughout the world and especially in the Southern Hemisphere, Pope Francis is the first non-European pope in almost 1,300 years. He is also the first Jesuit pope. Pope Francis comes with a different background and set of experiences. Both as archbishop and as pope, his flock knows him for his humility, ascetic frugality in solidarity with the poor, and closeness. He was born in Buenos Aires to a family of Italian immigrants, earned a diploma in chemistry, and followed a priestly vocation in the Jesuit order after an experience of God's mercy while receiving the sacrament of Reconciliation. Even though he is known for his smile and humor, the world also recognizes Pope Francis as a stern figure that stands against the evils of the world and challenges powerful government officials, when necessary.

The Church he leads is one that has been burdened in the West by the aftermath of sex abuse scandals and increased secularism. It is also a Church that is experiencing shifting in numbers out of the West and is being challenged with religious persecution in the Middle East, Asia, and Africa. The Vatican that Pope Francis has inherited is plagued by cronyism and scandal. This Holy Father knows, however, that his job is not merely about numbers, politics, or even success. He steers clear of pessimism knowing that he is the head of Christ's Body on earth and works with Christ's grace. This is the man God has chosen in these times to lead his flock.

# Chapter 2: Early Life in Argentina

Jorge Mario Bergoglio was born on December 17, 1936, in the Flores district of Buenos Aires. The district was a countryside locale outside the main city during the nineteenth century and many rich people in its early days called this place home. By the time Jorge was born, Flores was incorporated into the city of Buenos Aires and became a middle class neighborhood. Flores is also the home of the beautiful Romantic-styled Basilica of San José de Flores, built in 1831, with its dome over the altar, spire over the entrance, and columns at its facade. It was the Bergoglios' parish church and had much significance in Jorge's life.

Jorge's father's family had arrived in Argentina in 1929, immigrating from Piedimonte in northern Italy. They were not the only ones immigrating to the country. In the late nineteenth century, Argentina became industrialized and the government promoted immigration from Europe. During that time, the land prospered and Buenos Aires earned the moniker "Paris of the South." In the late nineteenth and early twentieth centuries waves of immigrants from Italy, Spain, and other European countries came off ships in the port of Buenos Aires. Three of Jorge's great uncles were the first in the family to immigrate to Argentina in 1922 searching for better employment opportunities after World War I. They established a paving company in Buenos Aires and built a four-story building for their company with the city's first elevator. Jorge's father and paternal grandparents followed the brothers in order to keep the family together and to escape Mussolini's fascist regime in Italy. Jorge's father and grandfather also helped with the business for a time. His father, Mario, who had been an accountant for a rail company in Italy, provided similar services for the family business (Cardinal Bergoglio recalls more on the story of his family's immigration and his early life in Ch. 1 of Conversations with Jorge Bergoglio).

Providentially, the Bergoglios were long delayed in liquidating their assets in Italy; this forced them to miss the ship they planned to sail on, the doomed Pricipessa Mafalda, which sank off the northern coast of Brazil before reaching Buenos Aires. The family took the Giulio Cesare instead and arrived safely in Argentina with Jorge's Grandma Rosa. Grandma Rosa wore a fur coat stuffed with the money the family brought with them from Italy. Economic hard times eventually hit Argentina in 1932 and the family's paving business went under, but the Bergoglio brothers began anew.

Jorge's father, Mario, met his mother Regina at Mass in 1934. Regina was born in Argentina, but her parents were also Italian immigrants. Mario and Regina married the following year after meeting. Jorge, the eldest of their five children, was born in 1936. Jorge fondly recalls his mother gathering the children around the radio on Sunday afternoons to listen to opera and explain the story. A true porteño, as the inhabitants of the port city of Buenos Aires are called, Jorge liked to play soccer, listen to Latin music, and dance the tango. Jorge's paternal grandparents lived around the corner from his home. He greatly admired his Grandma Rosa, and keeps her written prayer for her grandchildren with him until this day. Jorge recalls that while his grandparents kept their personal conversations in Piedmontese, Mario chose mostly to speak Spanish, preferring to look forward rather than back. Still, Jorge grew up speaking both Italian and Spanish.

Upon entering secondary school at the age of thirteen, his father insisted that Jorge begin work even though the family, in their modest lifestyle, was not particularly in need of extra income. Mario Bergoglio wanted to teach the boy the value of work and found several jobs for him during his adolescent years. Jorge worked in a hosiery factory for several years as a cleaner and at a desk. When he entered technical school to study food chemistry, Jorge found a job working in a laboratory. He worked under a woman who always challenged him to do his work thoroughly. He remembers her, though, with both fondness and sorrow. Years later, she was kidnapped and murdered along with members of her family because of her political views during the Dirty War, a conflict in the 1970's and 80's between the military dictatorship and guerrilla fighters in which thousands of Argentineans disappeared.

Initially unhappy with his father's decision to make him work, Jorge recalls later in his life that work was a valuable formative experience for him that taught him responsibility, realism, and how the world operated. He learned that a person's self worth often comes from their work, which led him to become committed later in life to promote a just culture of work rather than simply encouraging charity or entitlement. He believes that people need meaningful work in order to thrive. During his boyhood through his priestly ministry, he experienced the gulf in Argentina between the poor and the well off, which left the poor having few opportunities for gainful employment.

At the age of twenty-one, Jorge became dangerously ill. He was diagnosed with severe pneumonia and cysts. Part of his upper right lung was removed, and each day Jorge endured the pain and discomfort of saline fluid pumped through his chest to clear his system. Jorge remembers that the only person that was able to comfort him during this time was a religious sister who had catechized him from childhood, Sister Dolores. She exposed him to the true meaning of suffering with this simple statement: "You are imitating Christ." This stuck with him, and his sufferings during that time served as a crucible for his character, teaching him how to distinguish what is important in life from what is not. He was being prepared for what God was calling him to do in life, his vocation.

Made in the USA
Las Vegas, NV
03 September 2022

54605186R10079